Floral Patterns REVERSE Coloring Book

This book belongs to:

....

....

....

Inspiration

There are no rules! But you can try some of these ideas.

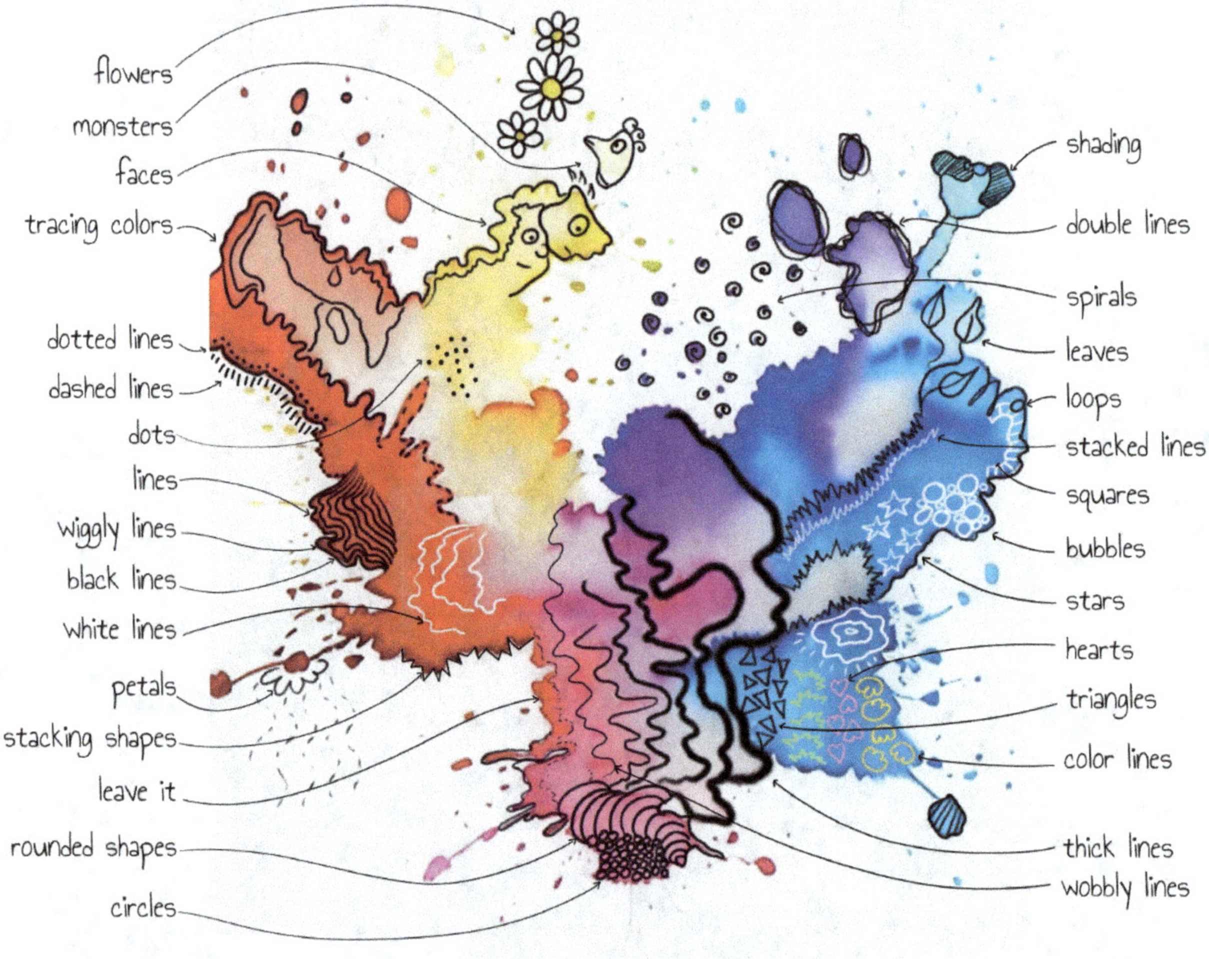
flowers
monsters
faces
tracing colors
dotted lines
dashed lines
dots
lines
wiggly lines
black lines
white lines
petals
stacking shapes
leave it
rounded shapes
circles
shading
double lines
spirals
leaves
loops
stacked lines
squares
bubbles
stars
hearts
triangles
color lines
thick lines
wobbly lines

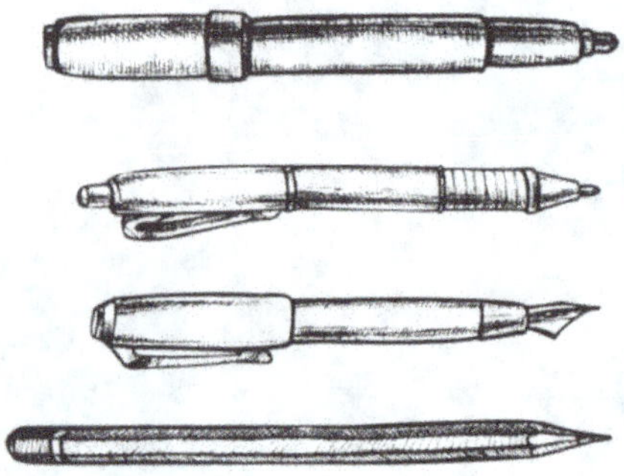

You can use any tool you like. Experiment with different thicknesses, textures and colors. Find out which one you like the most. You`ll be suprised by the effect.

Sample drawing

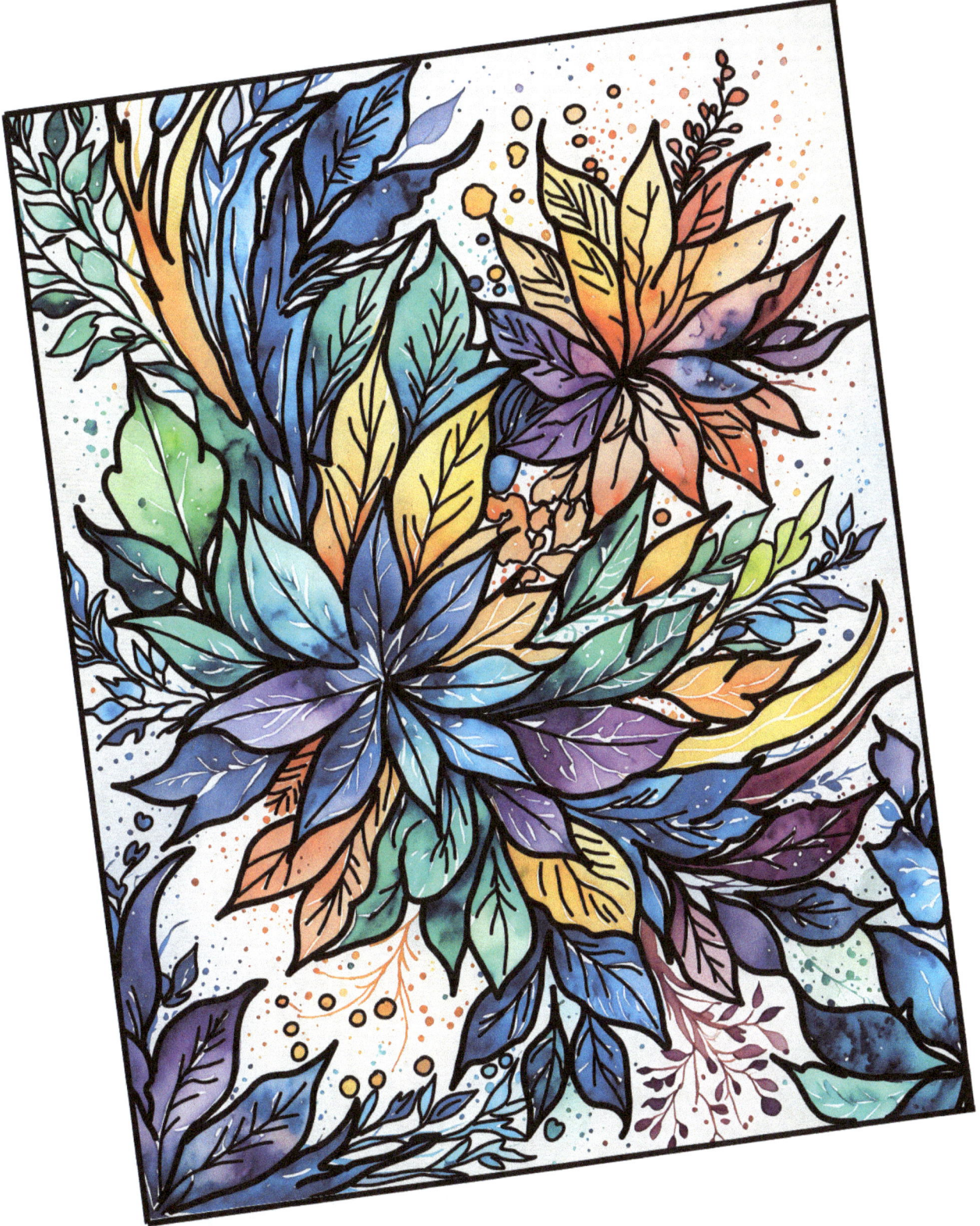

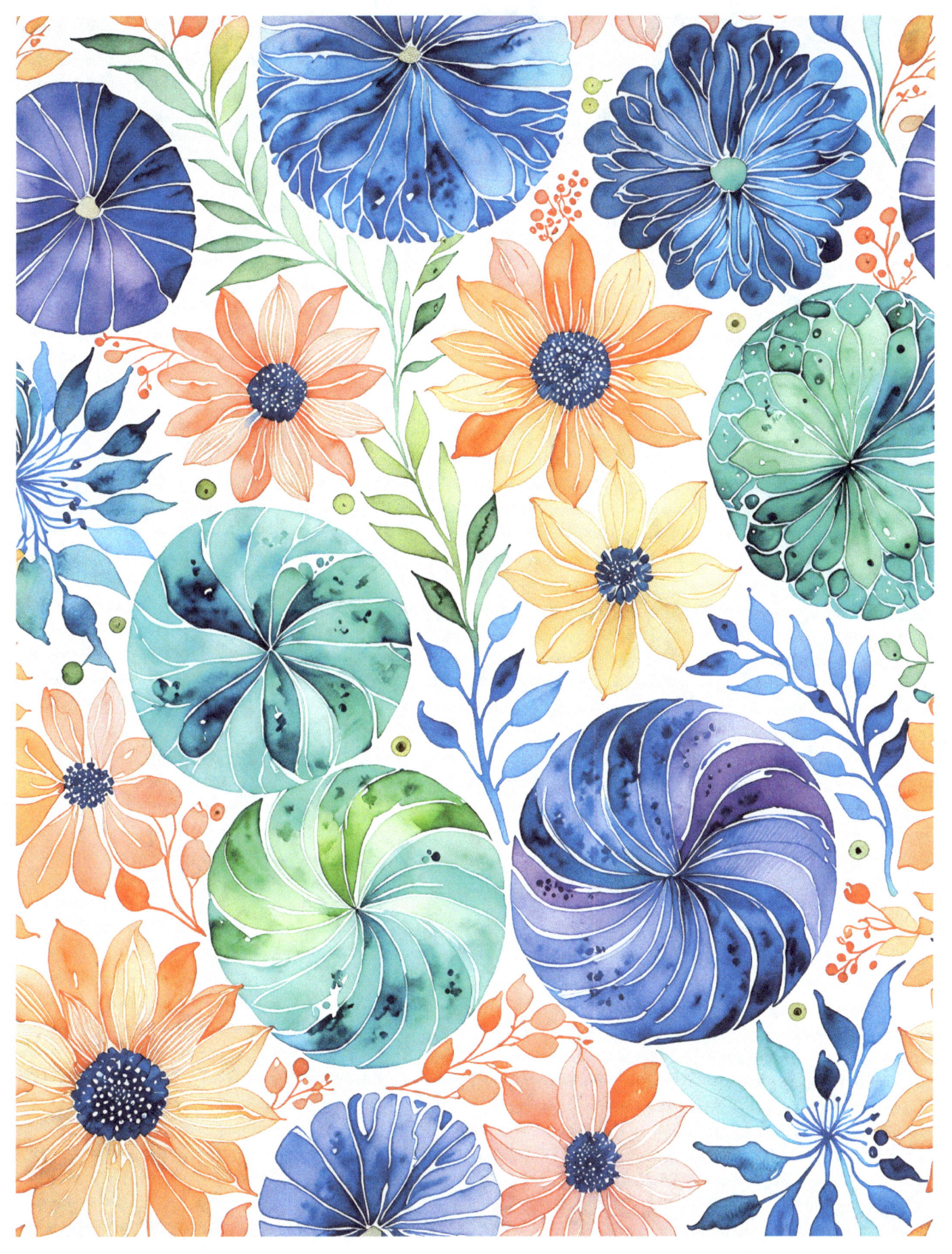

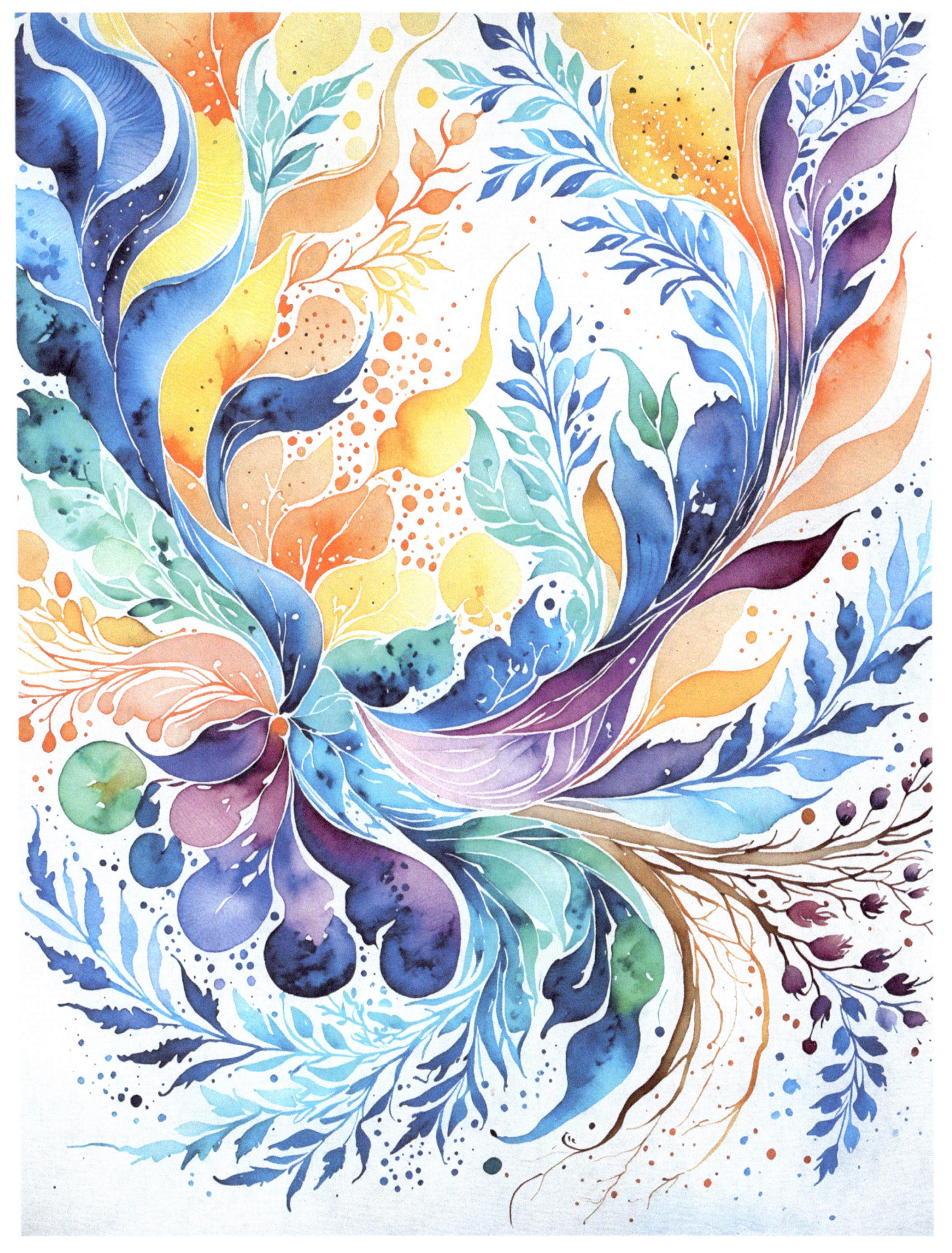

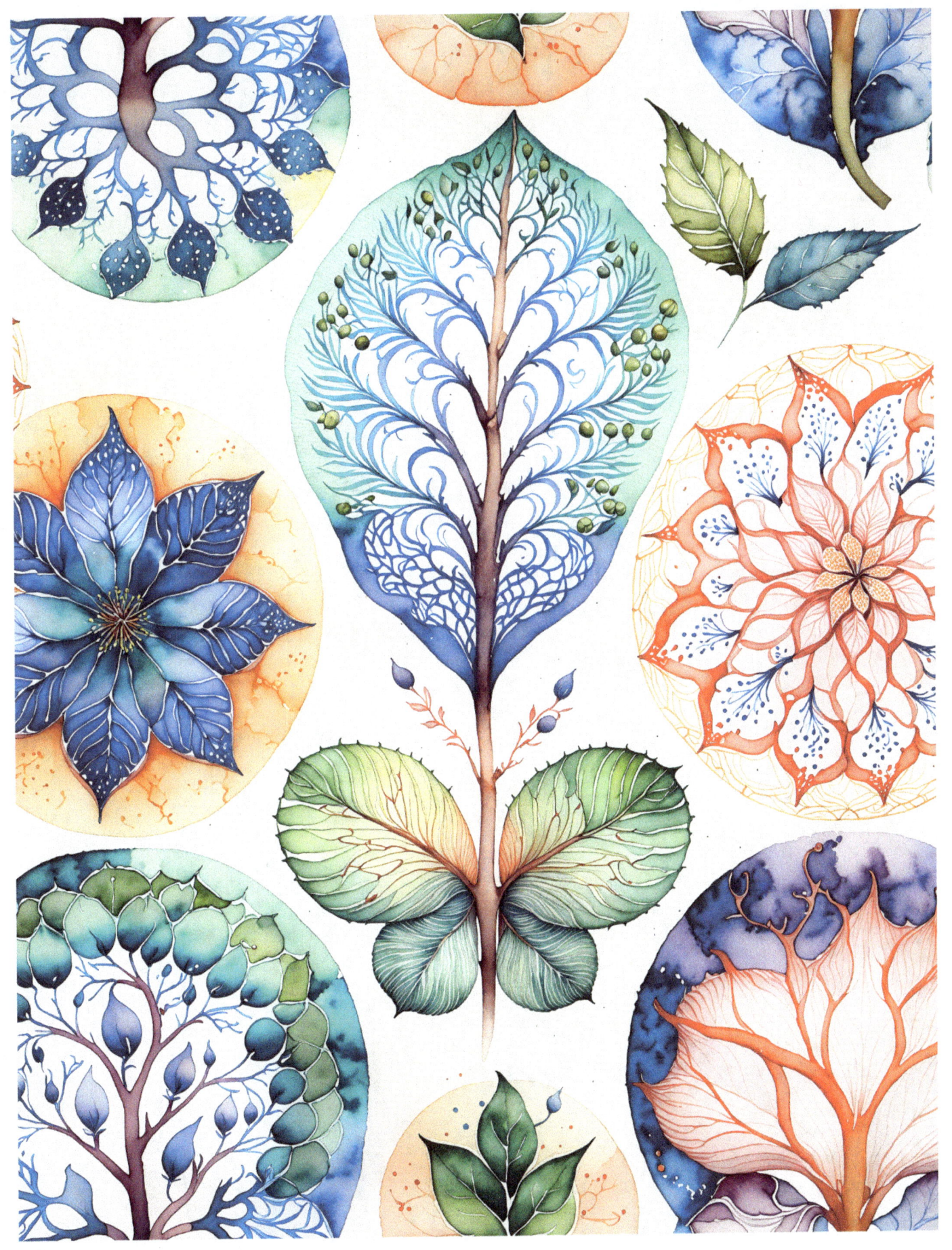

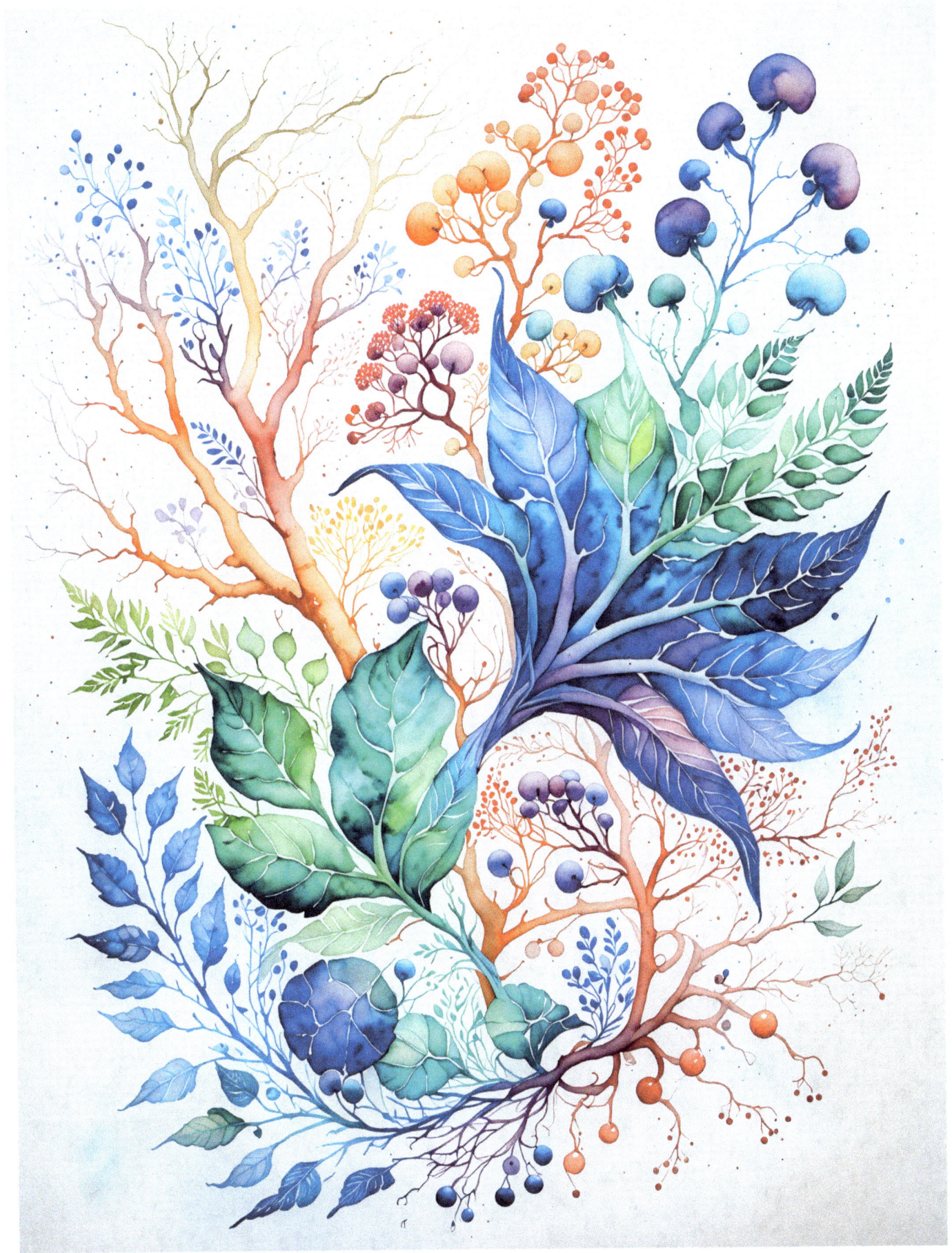

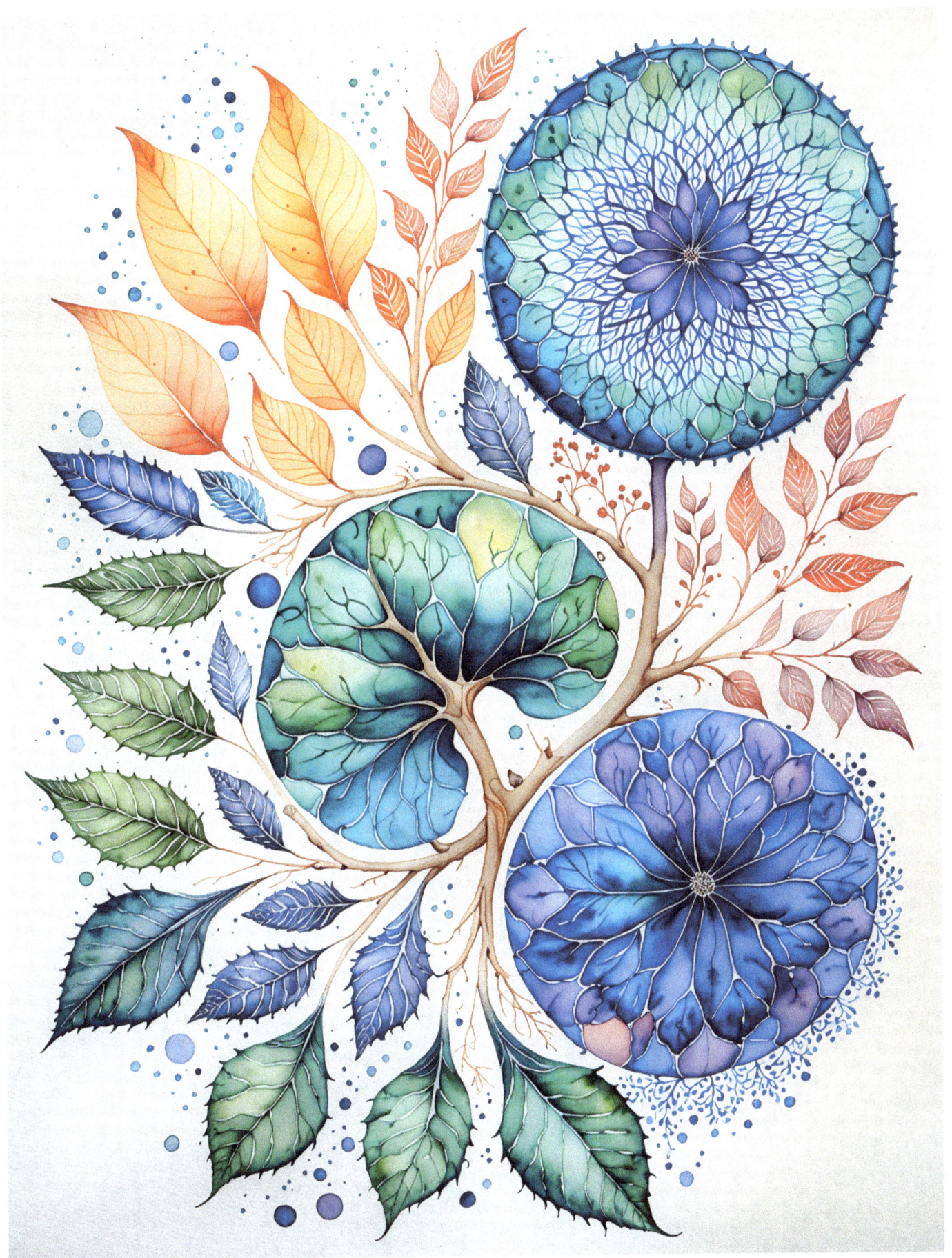

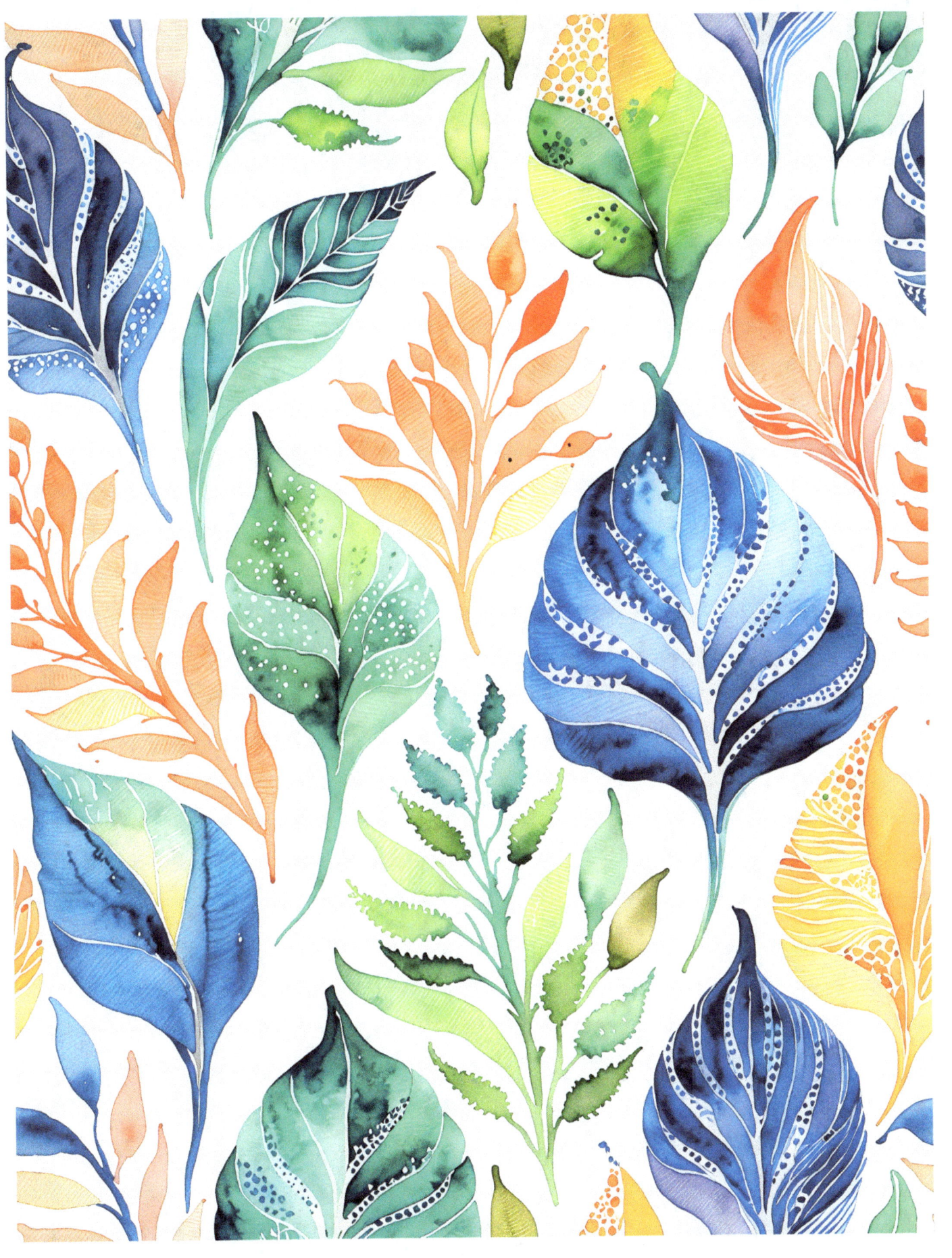

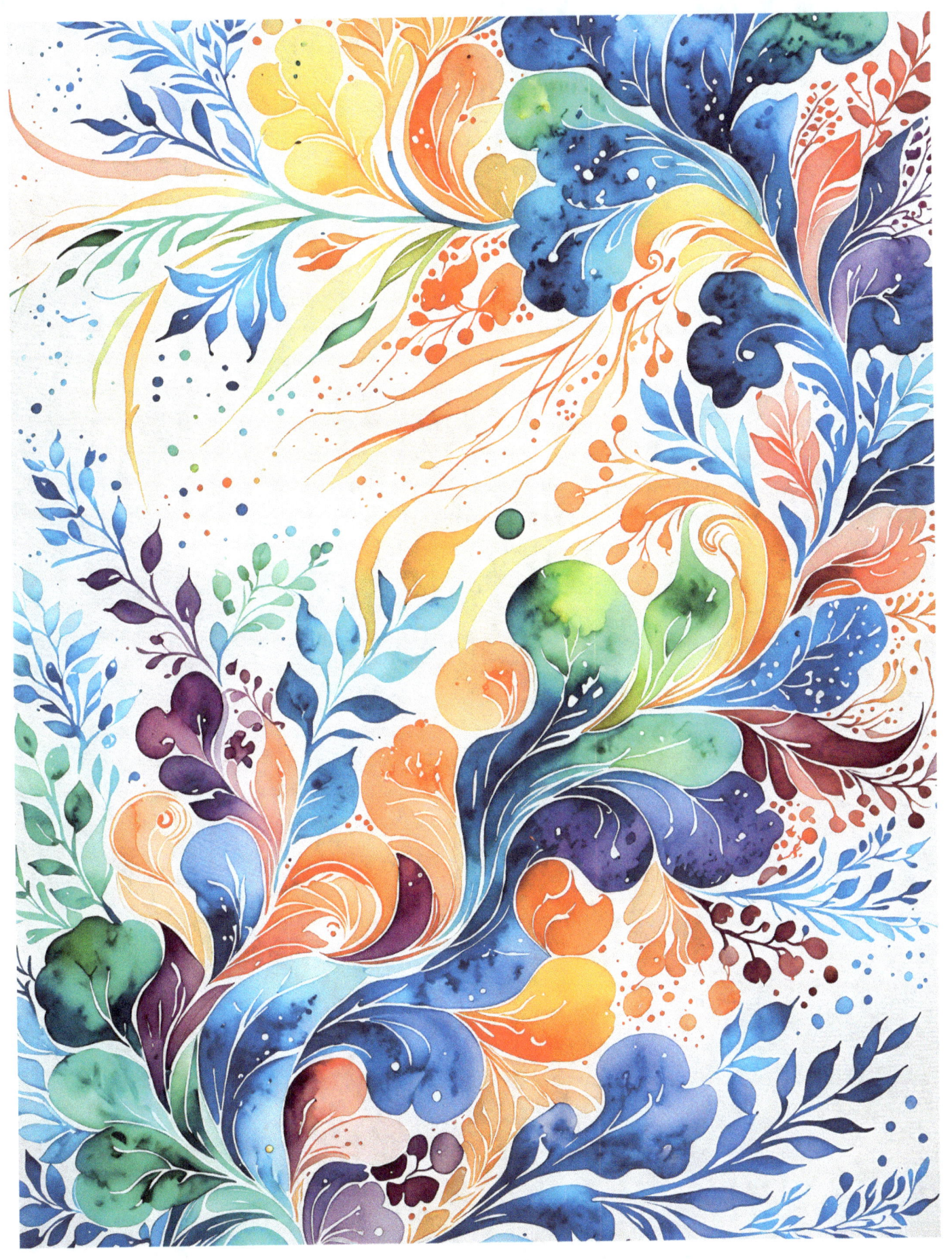

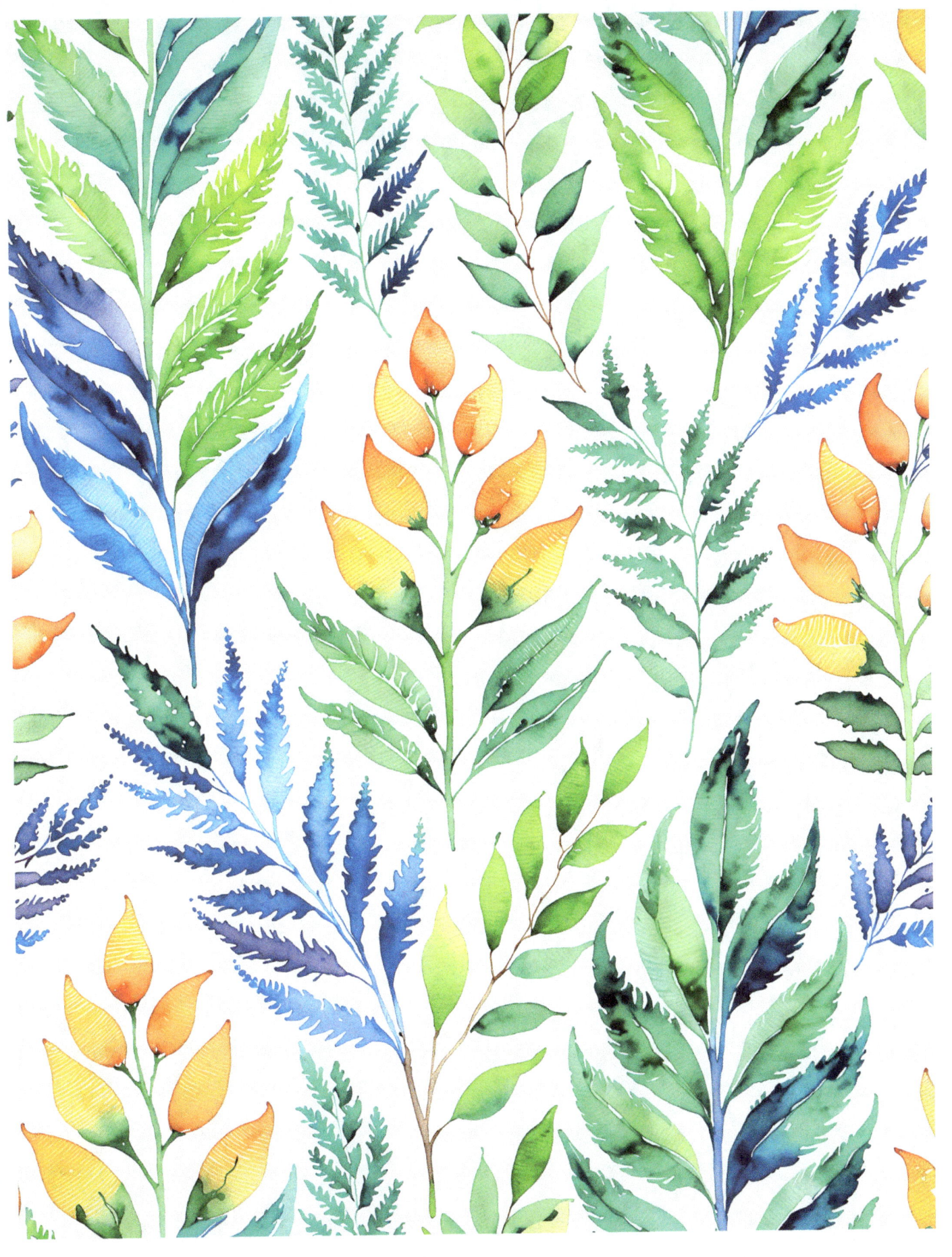

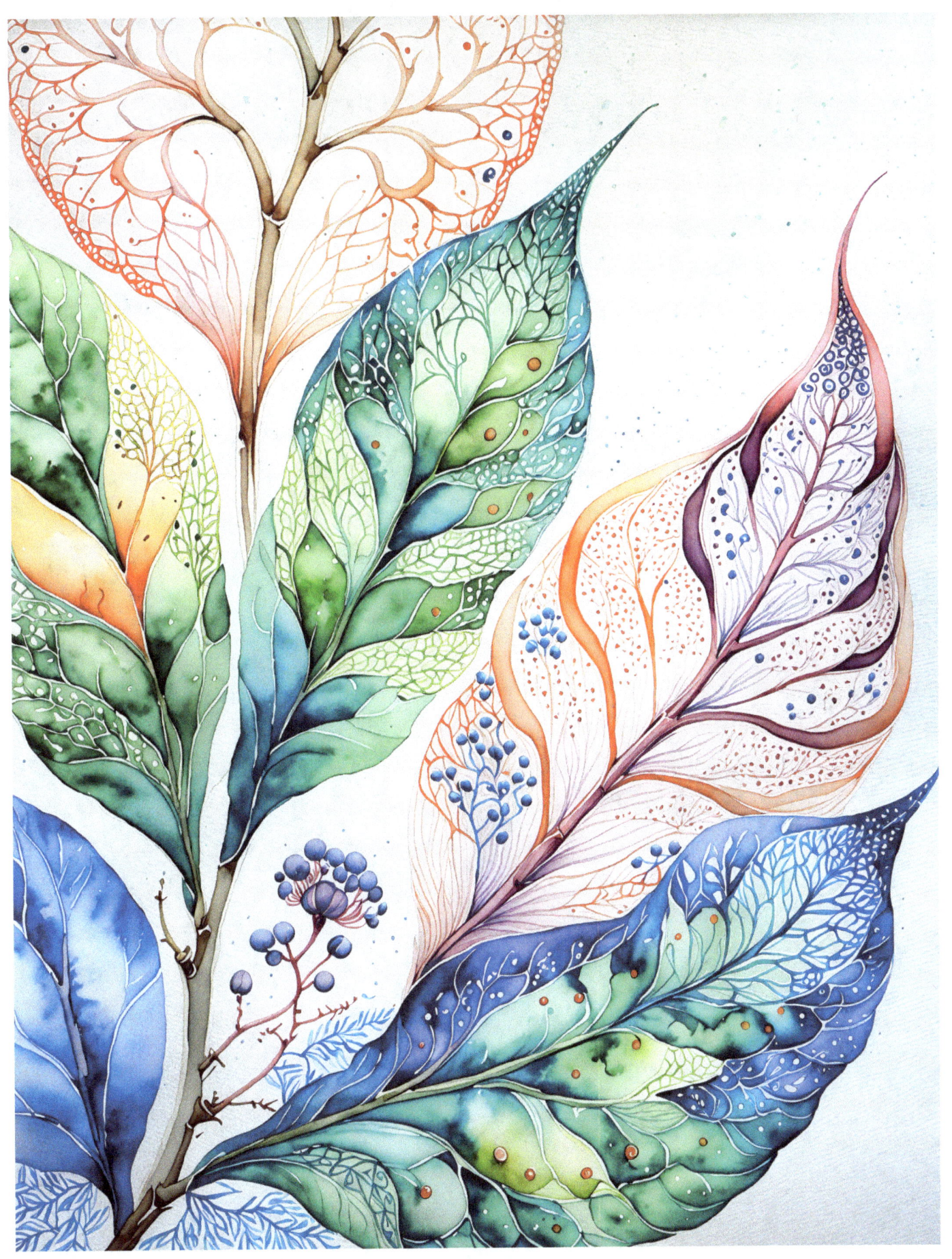

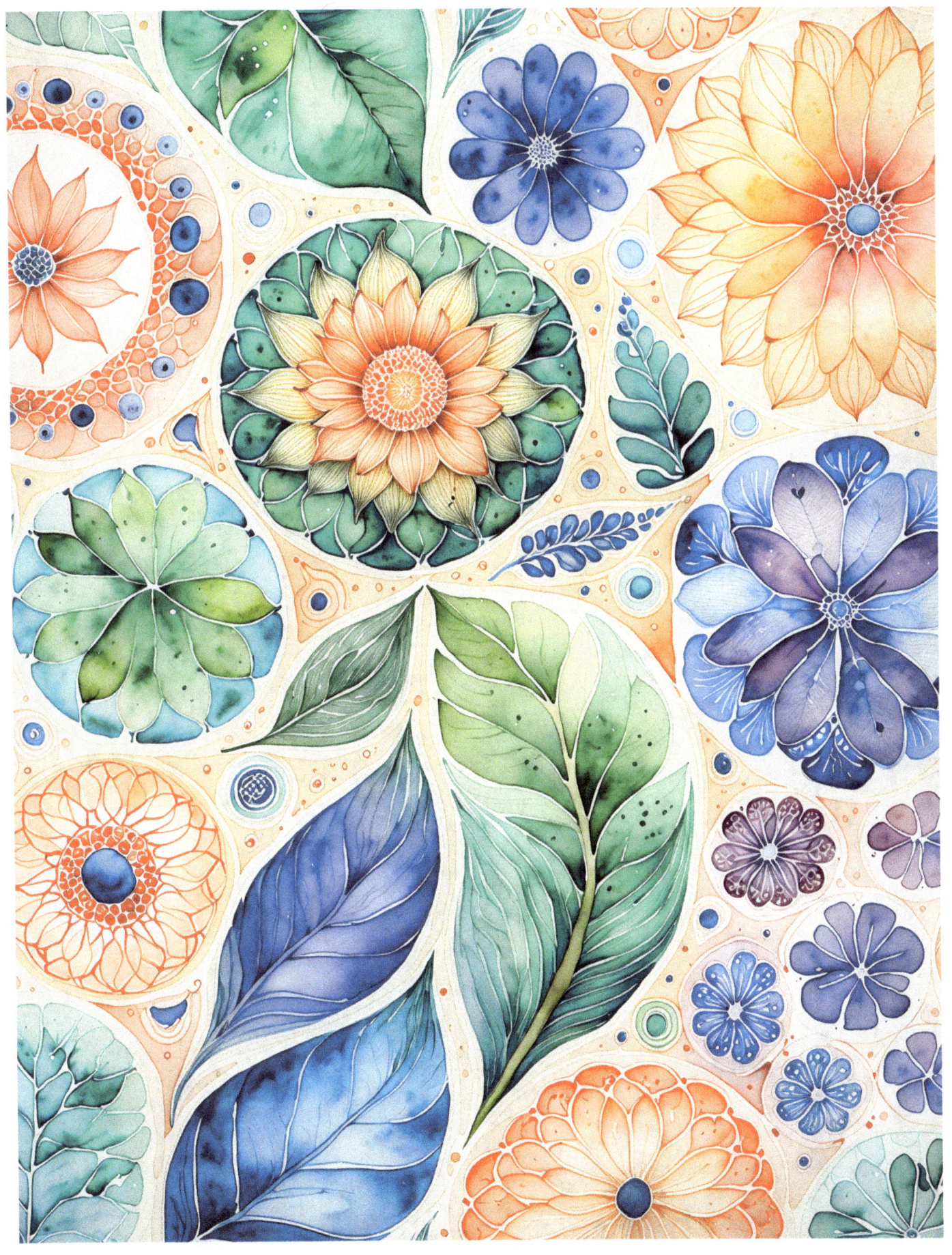

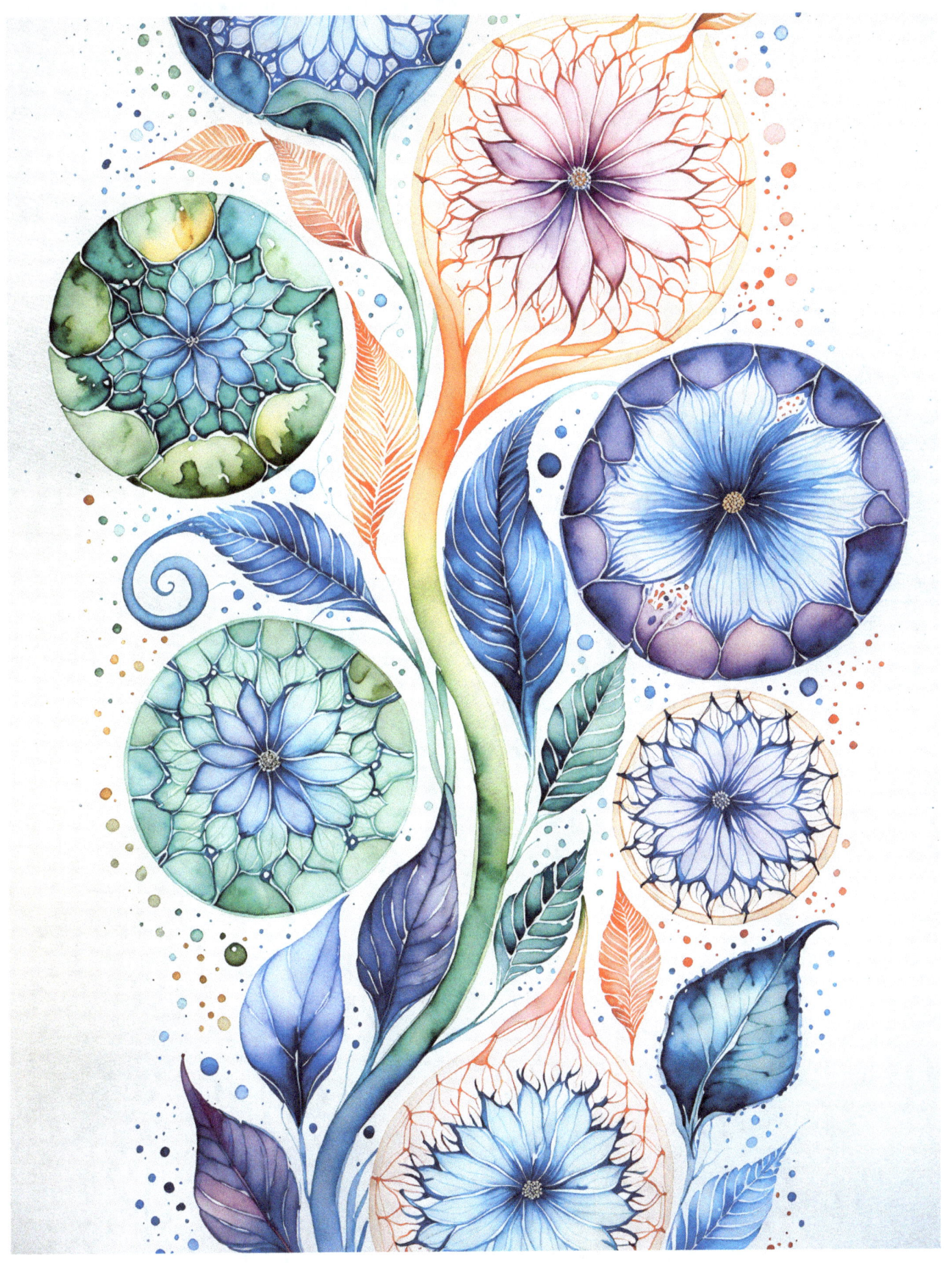

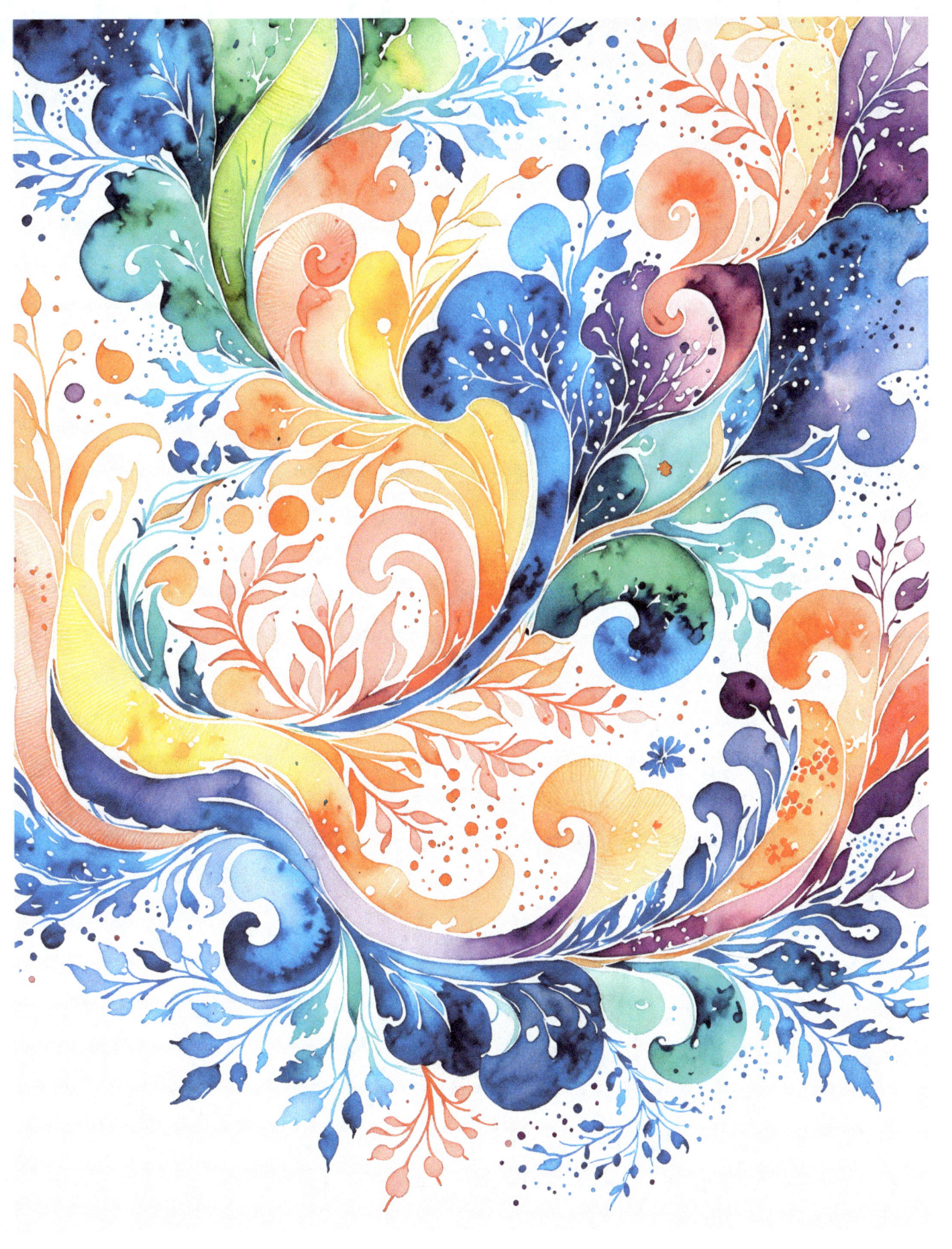

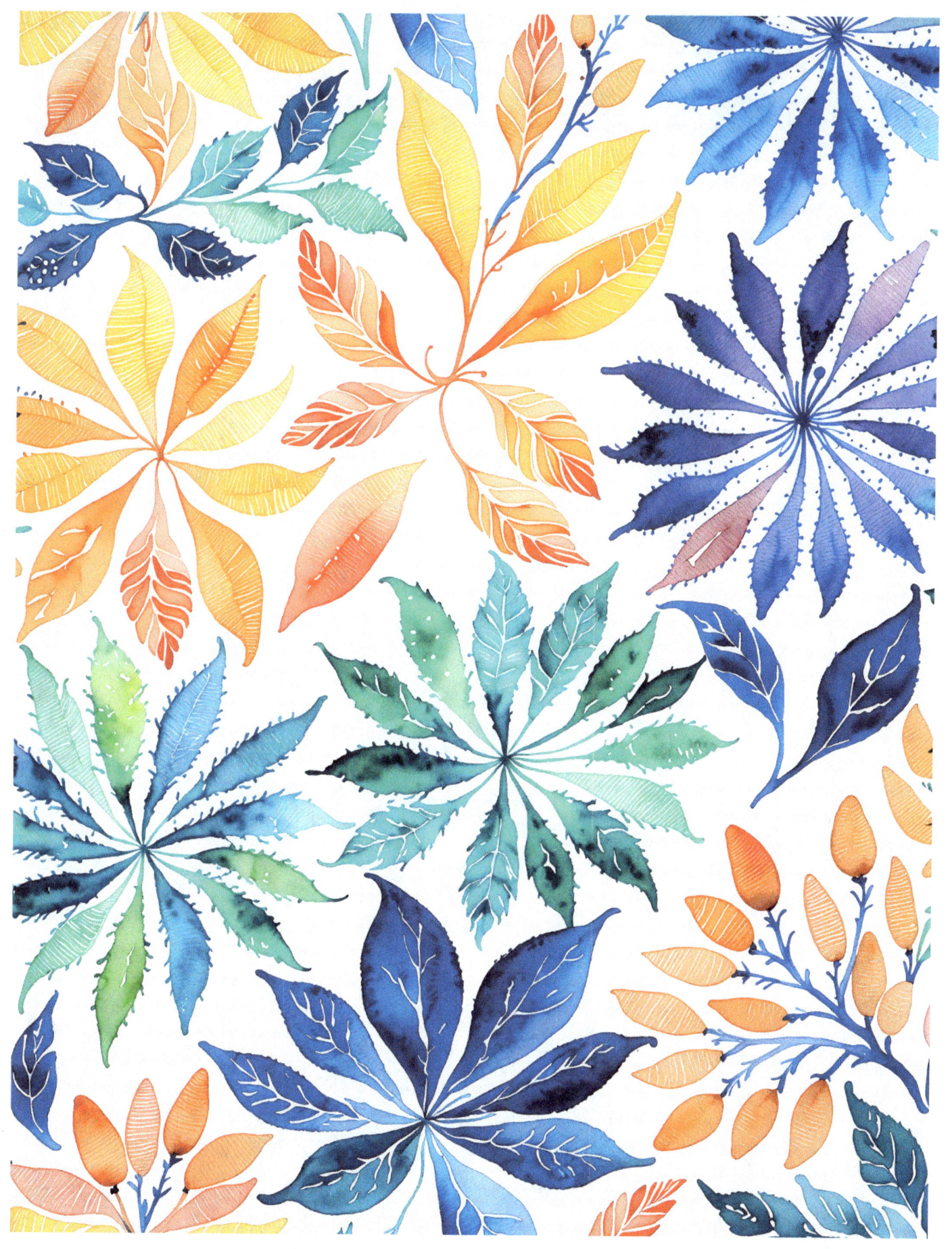

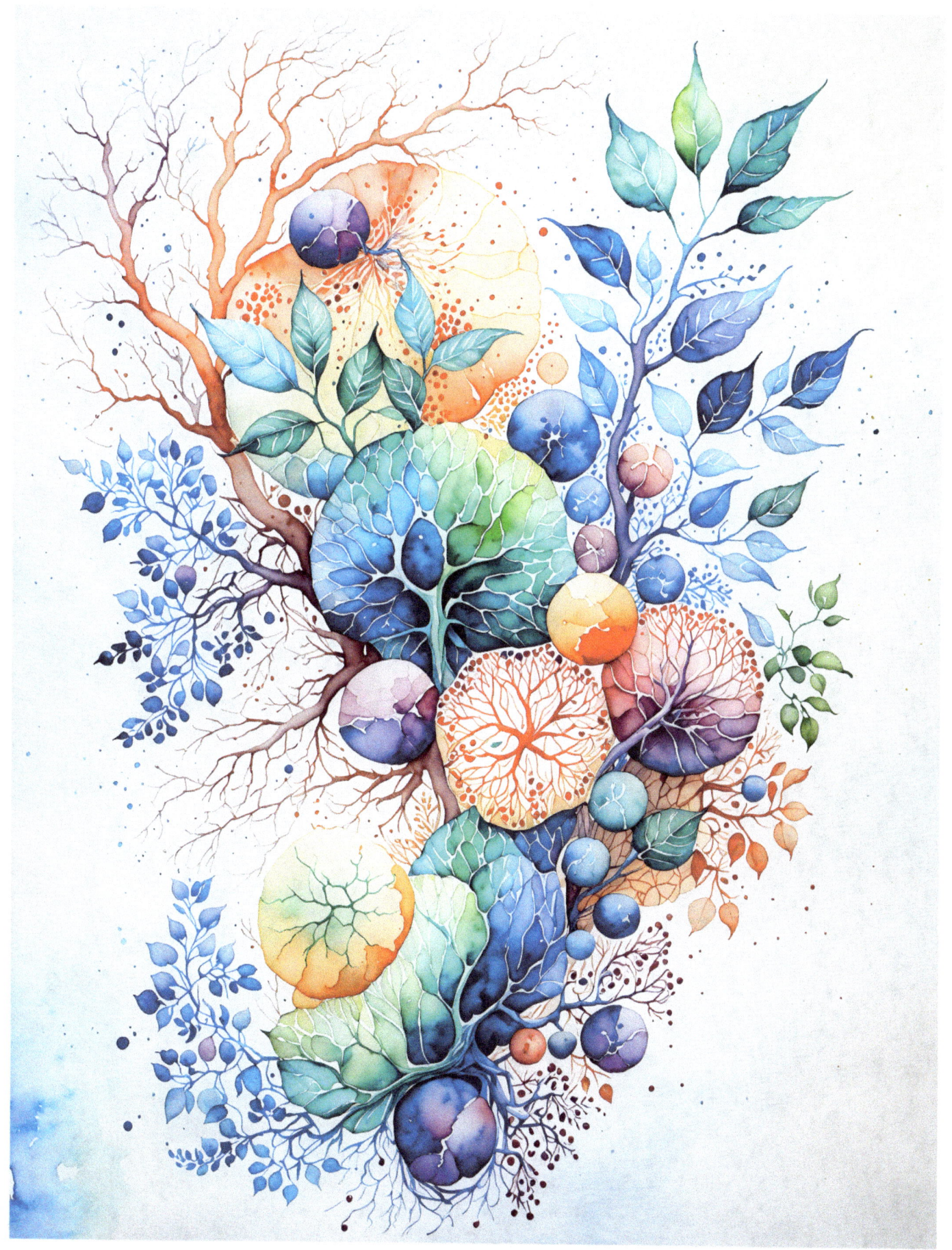

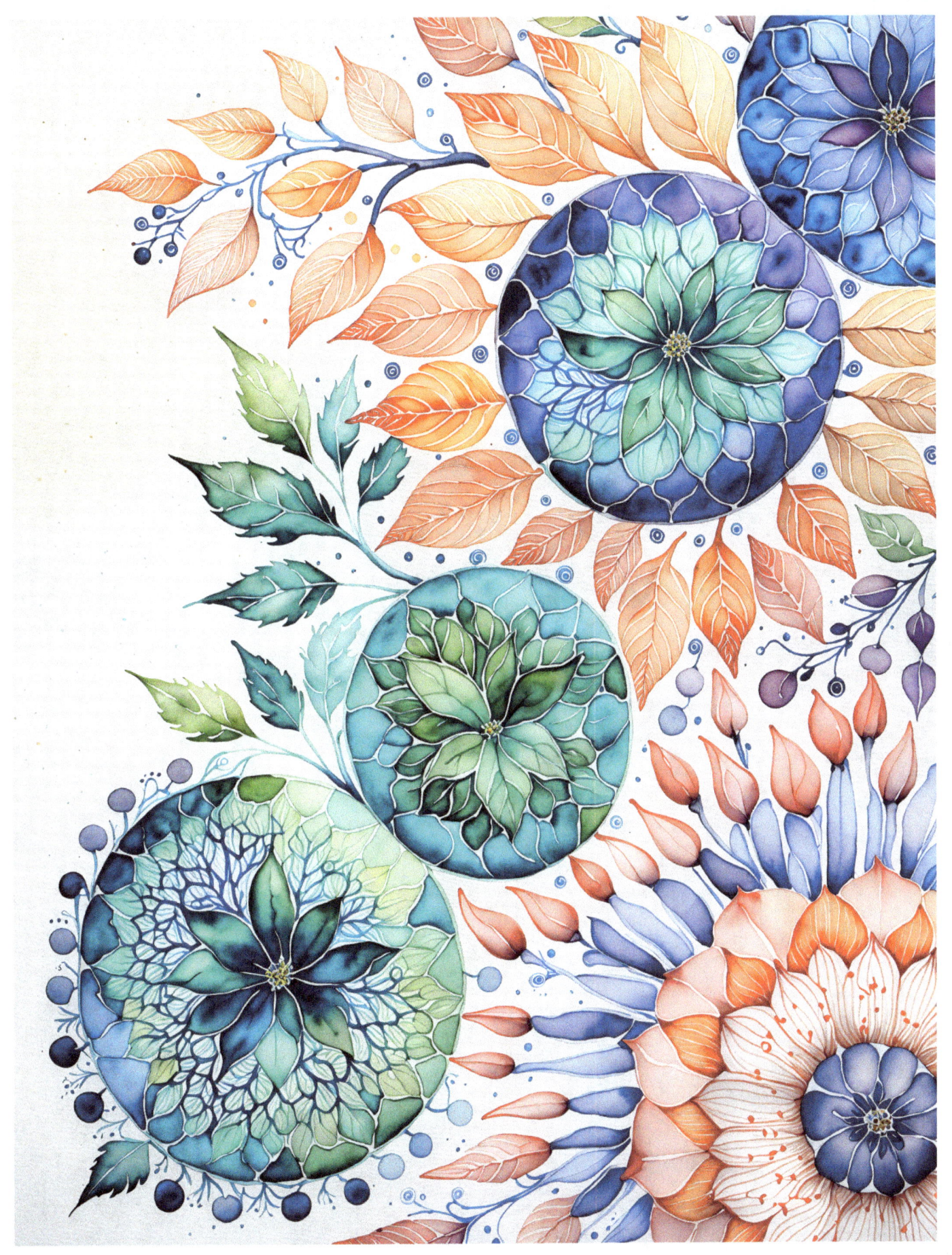

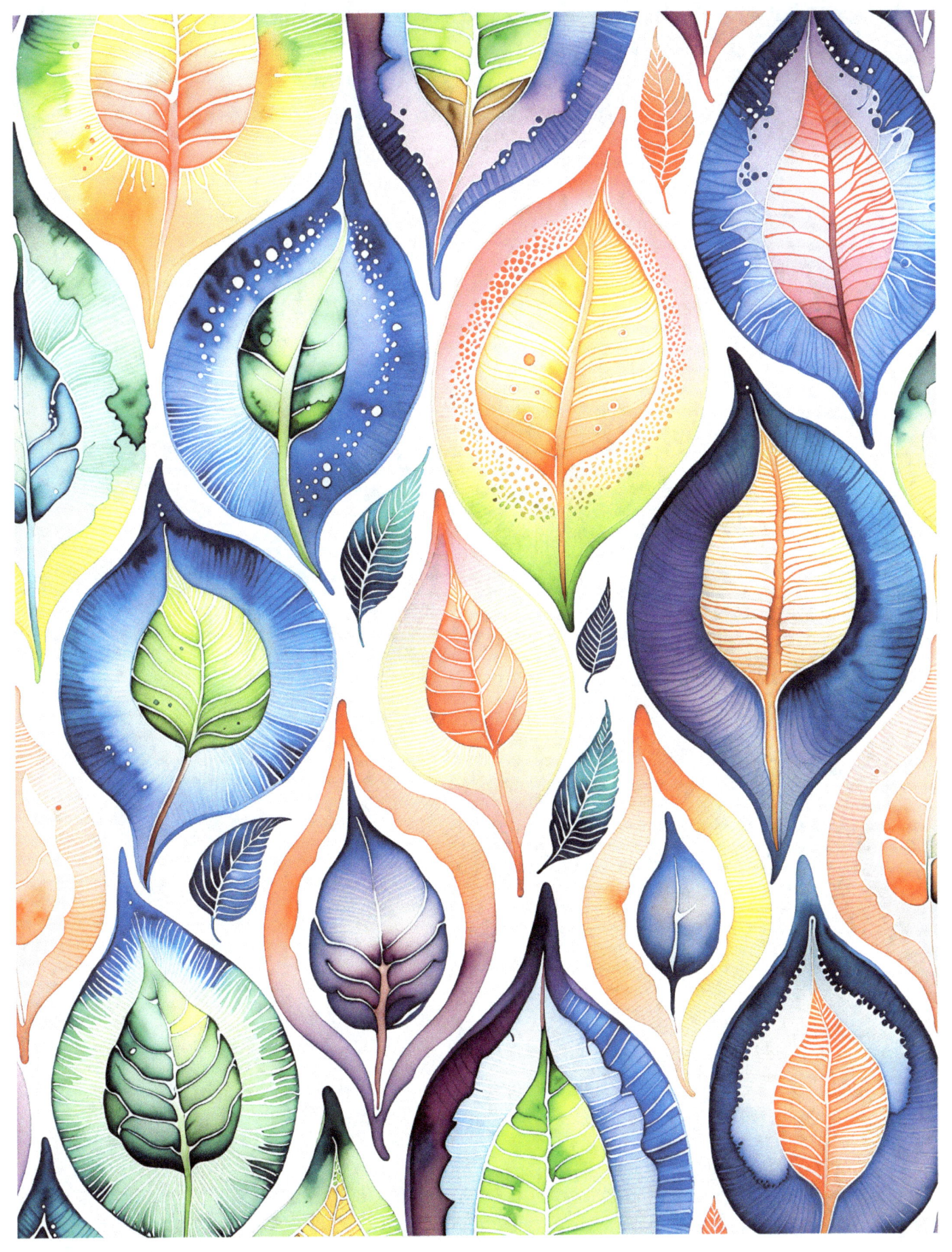

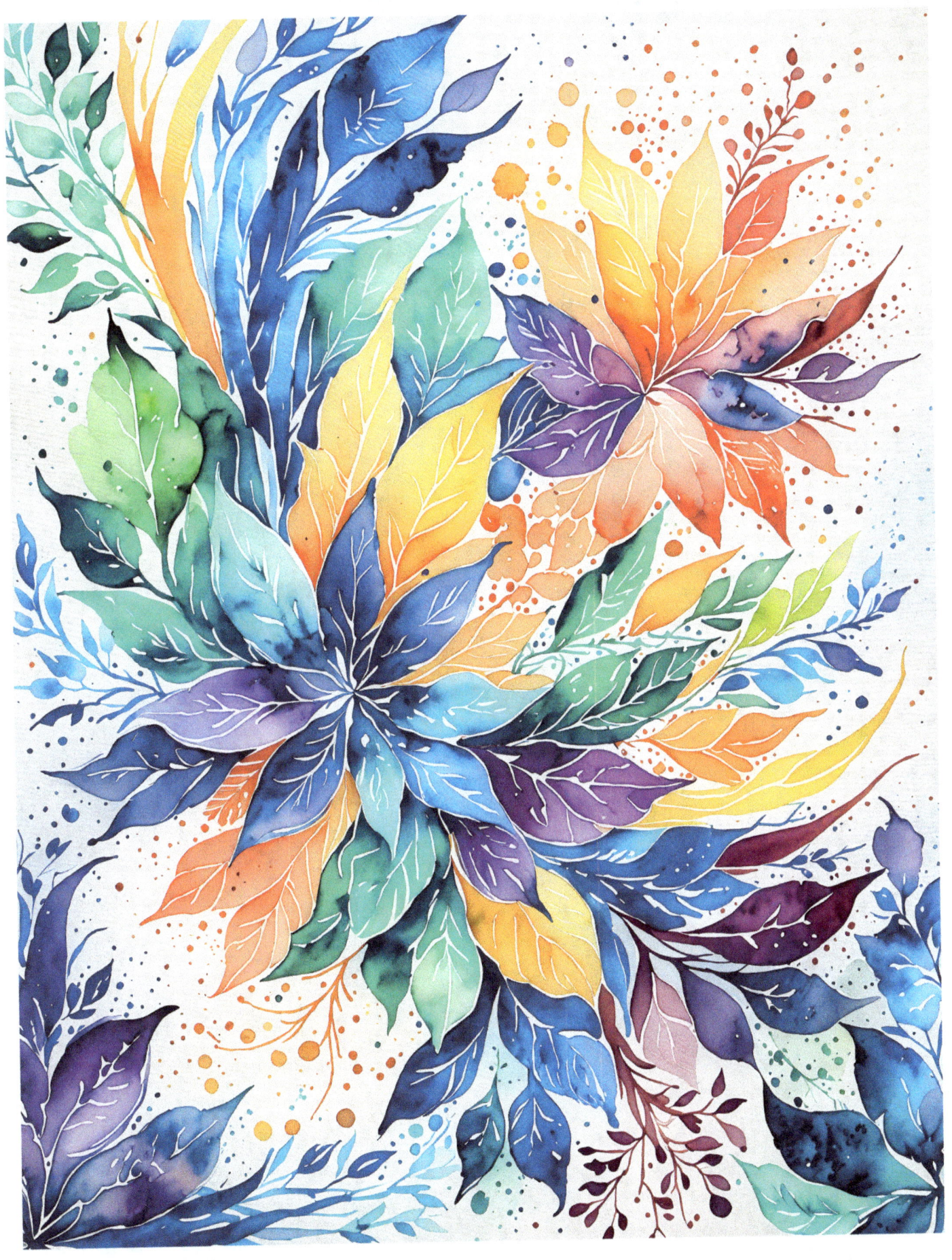

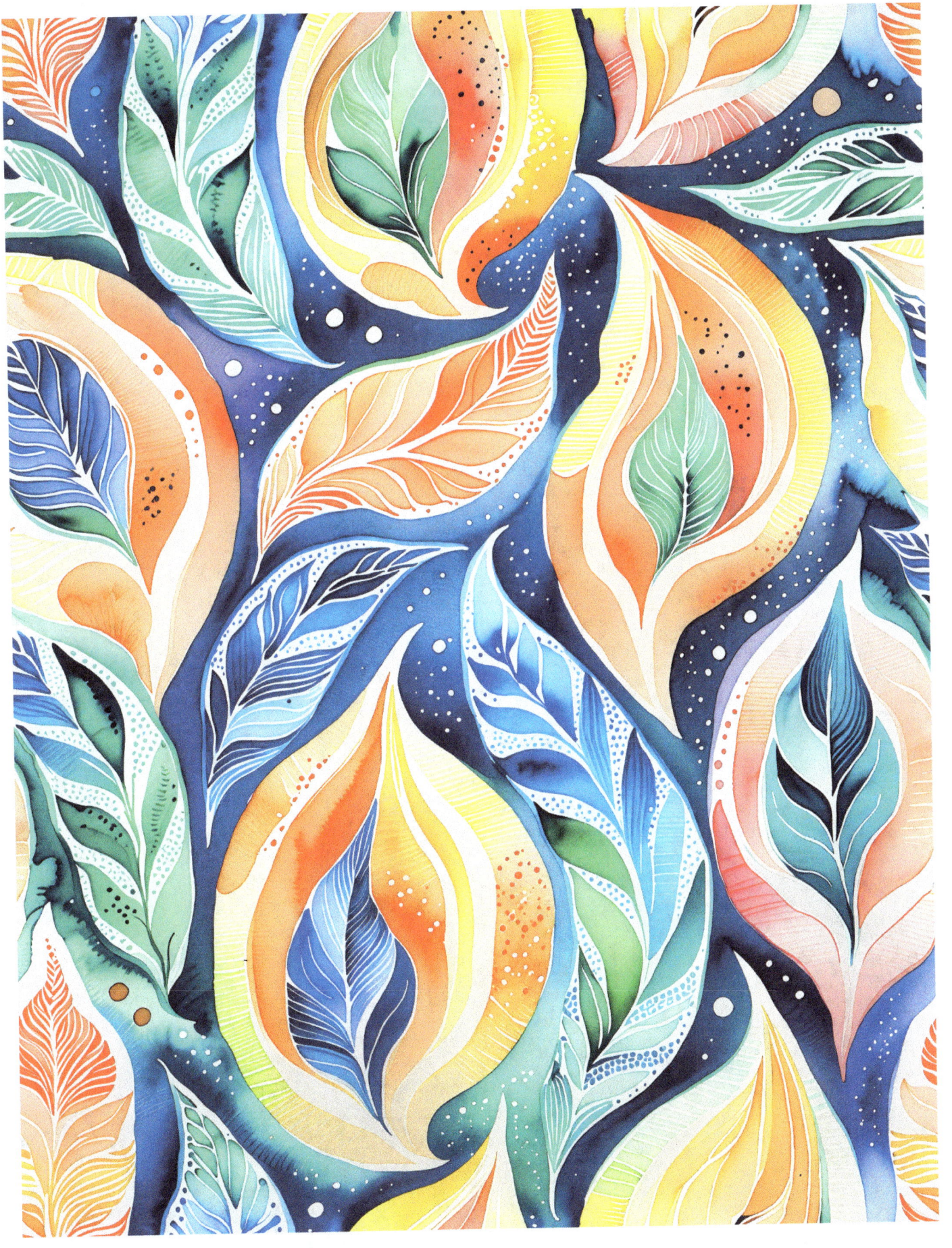

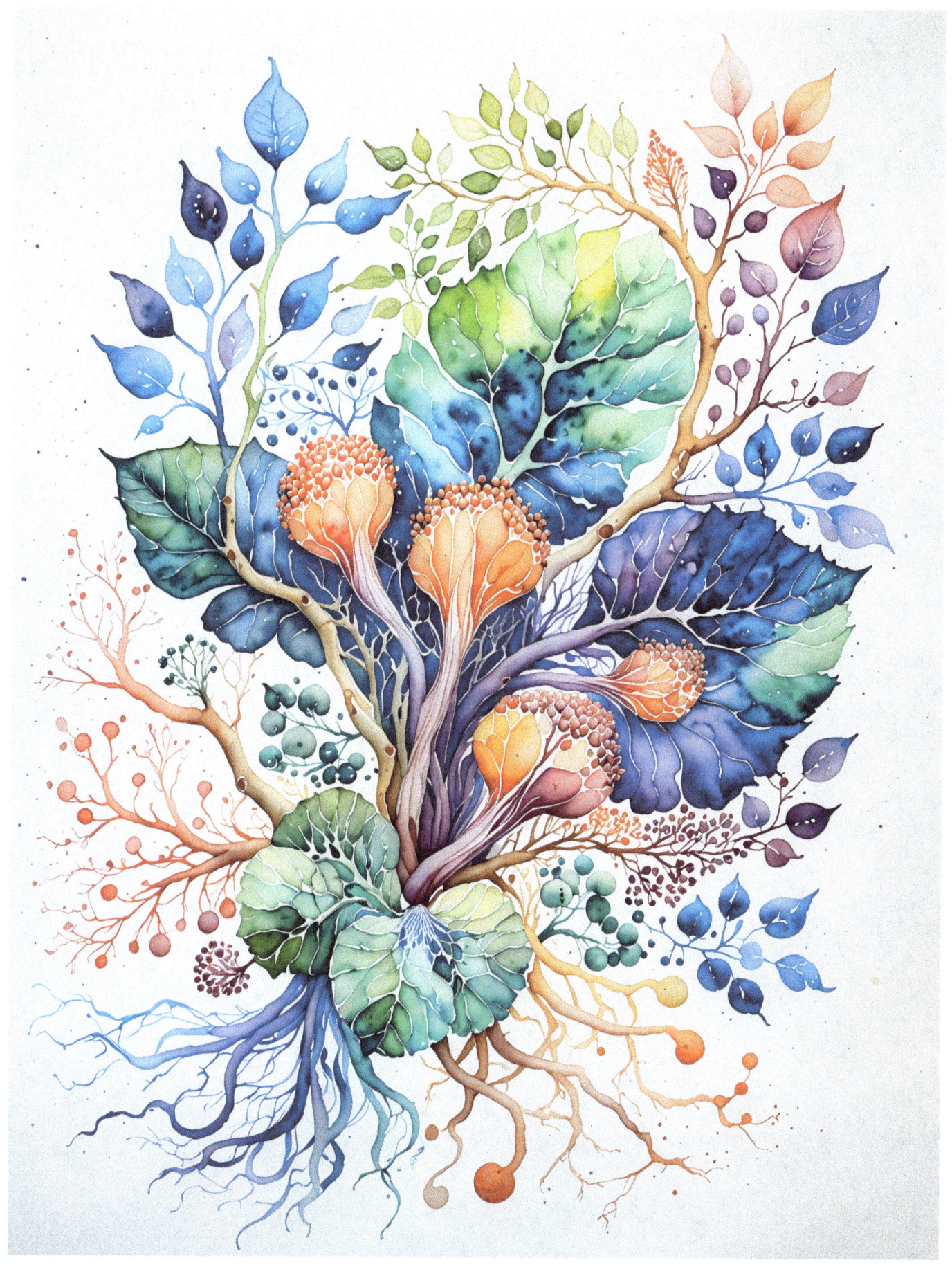

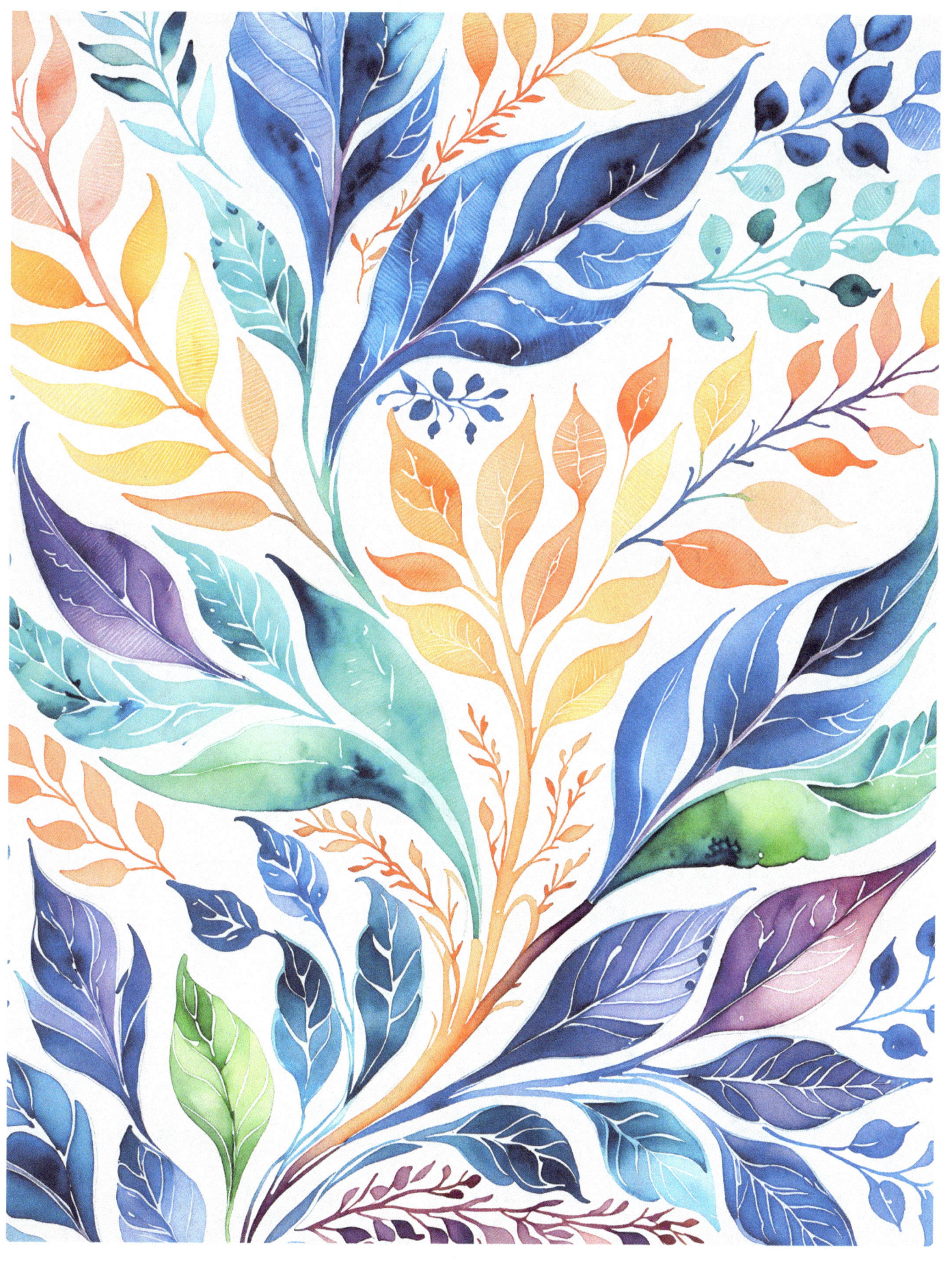

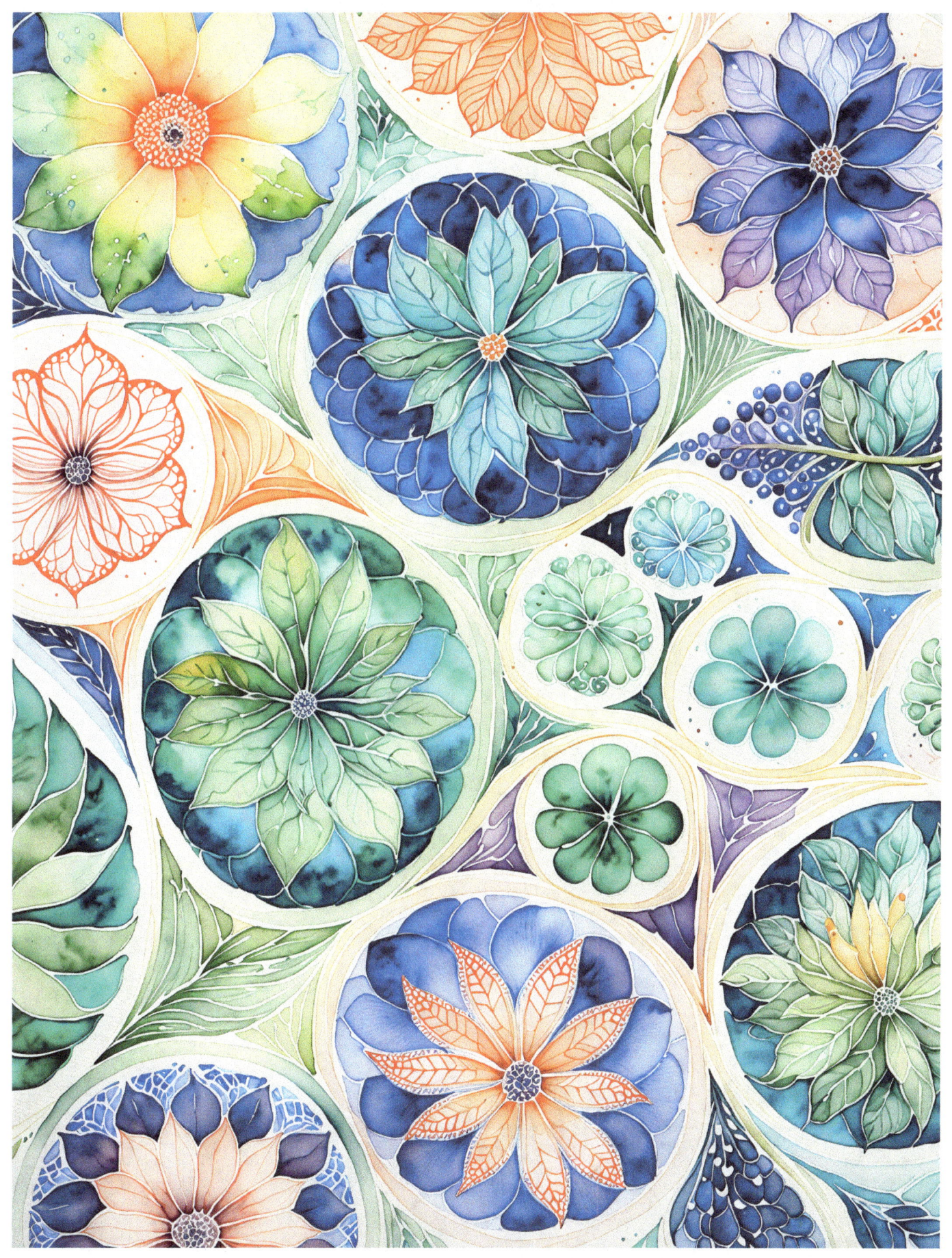

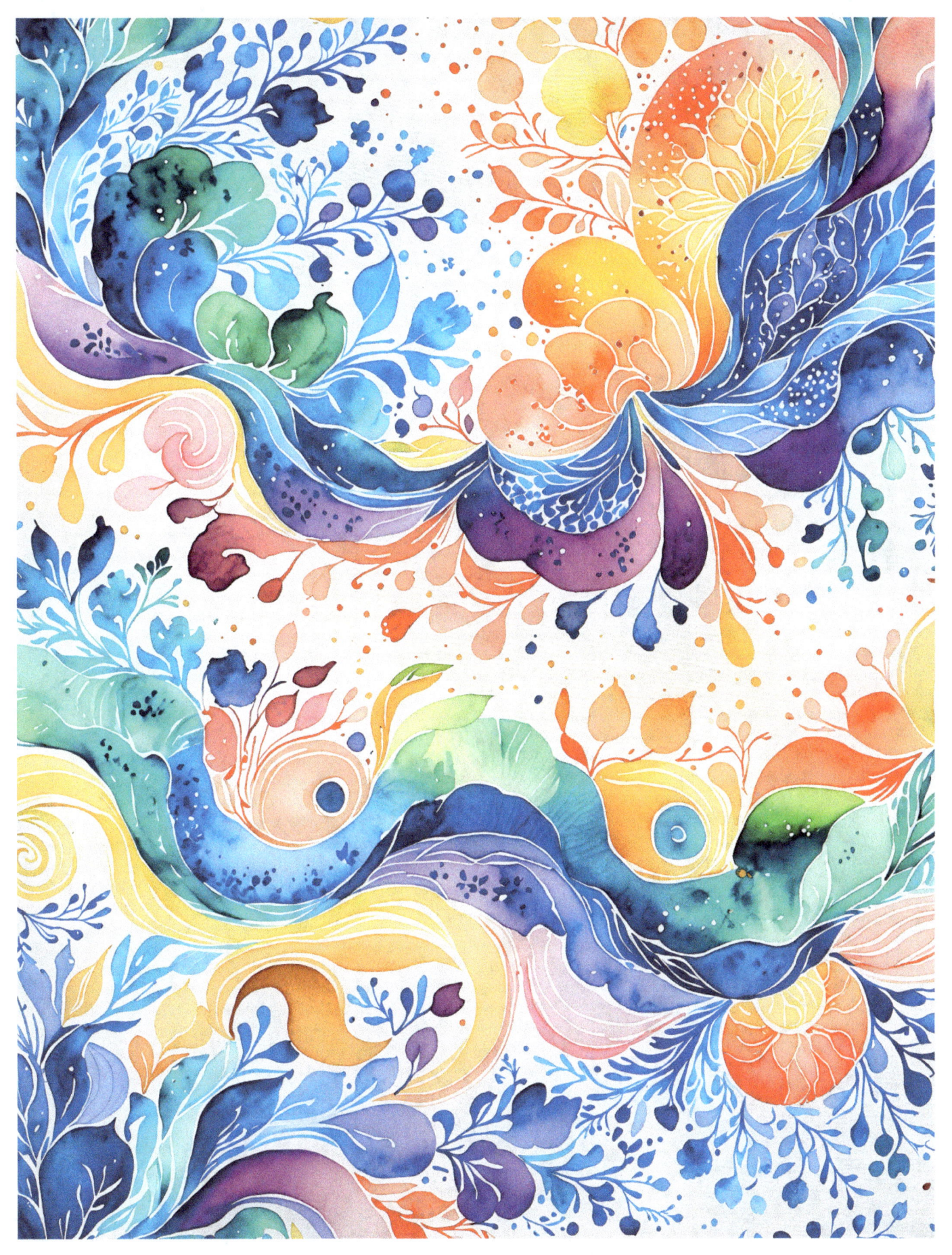

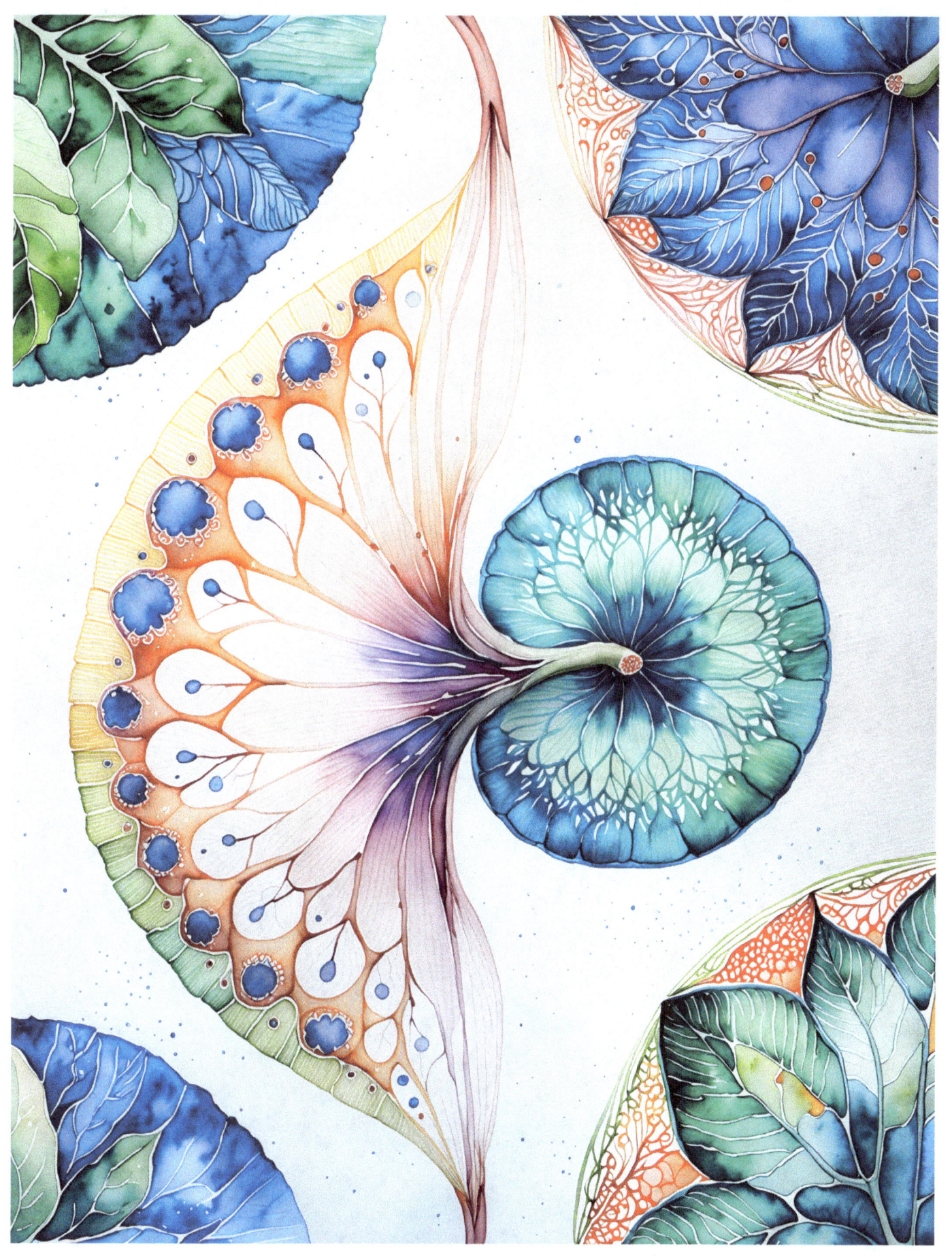

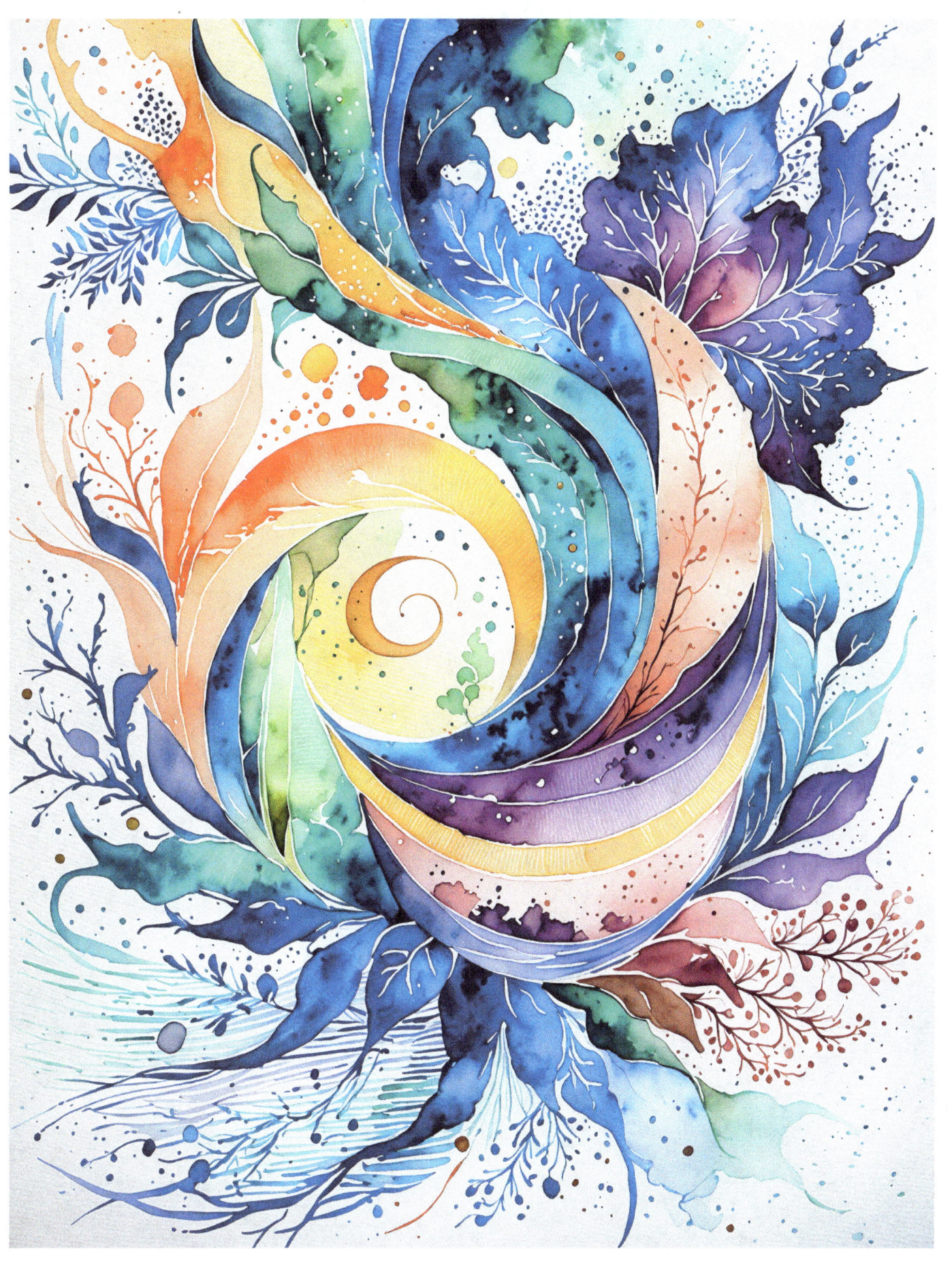

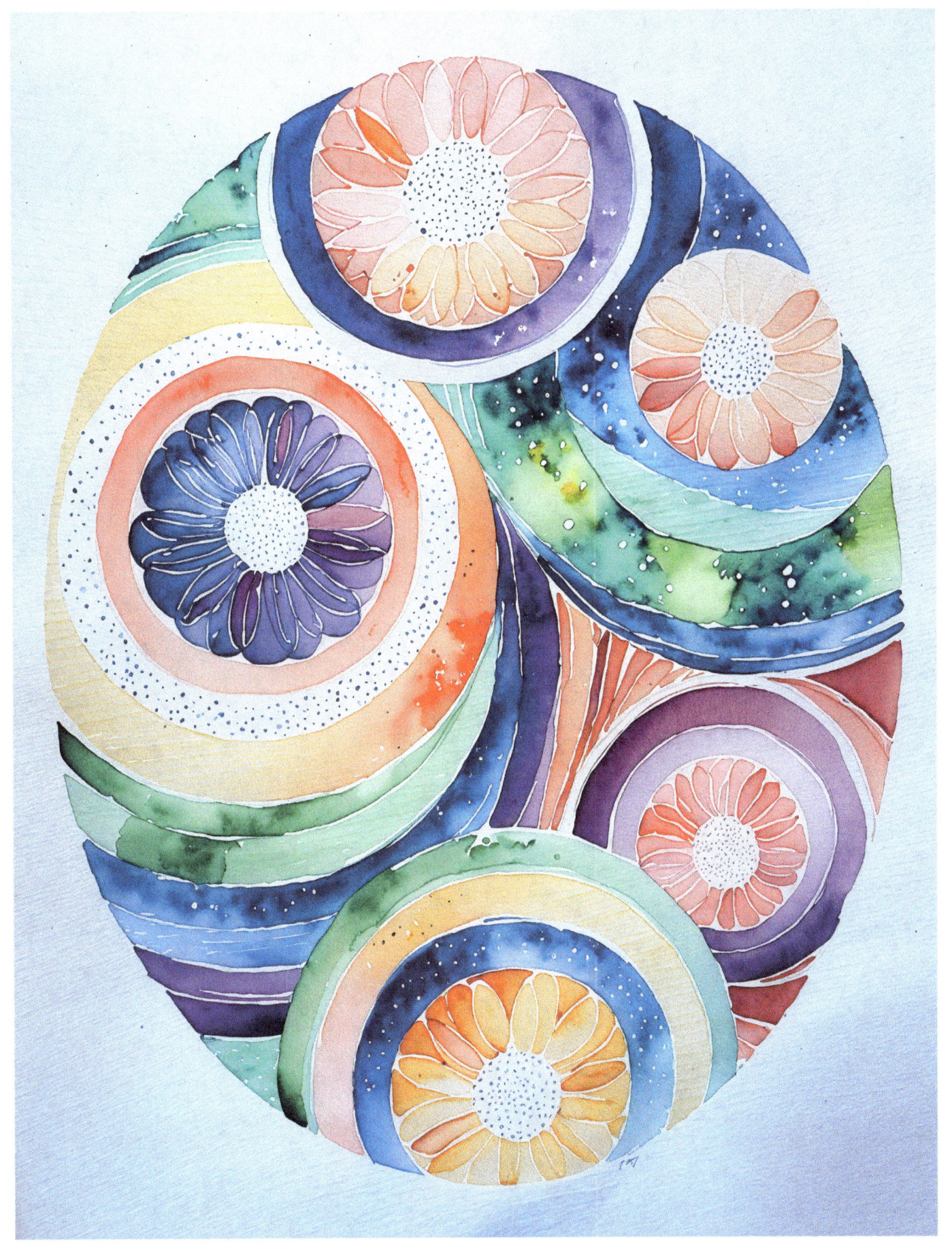

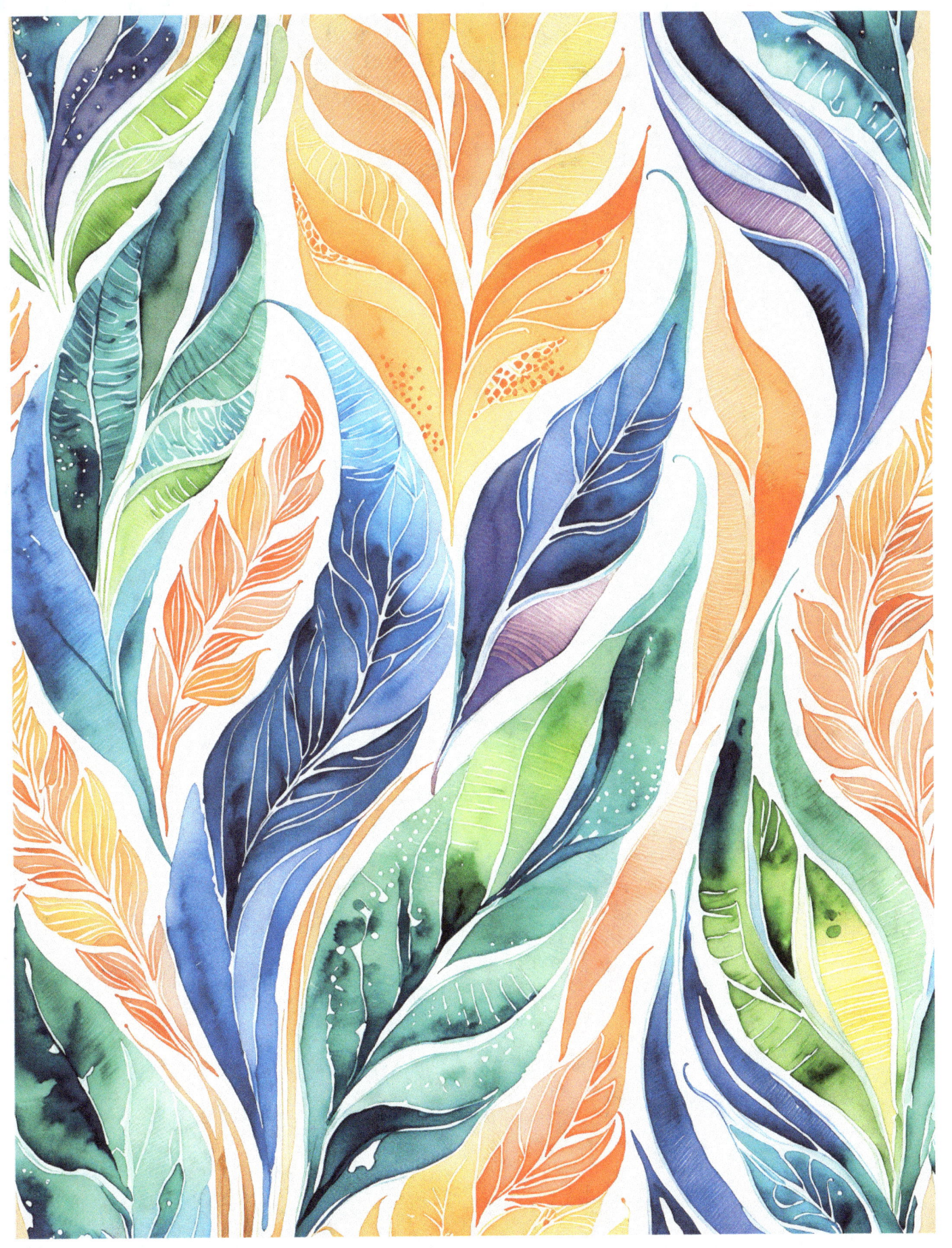

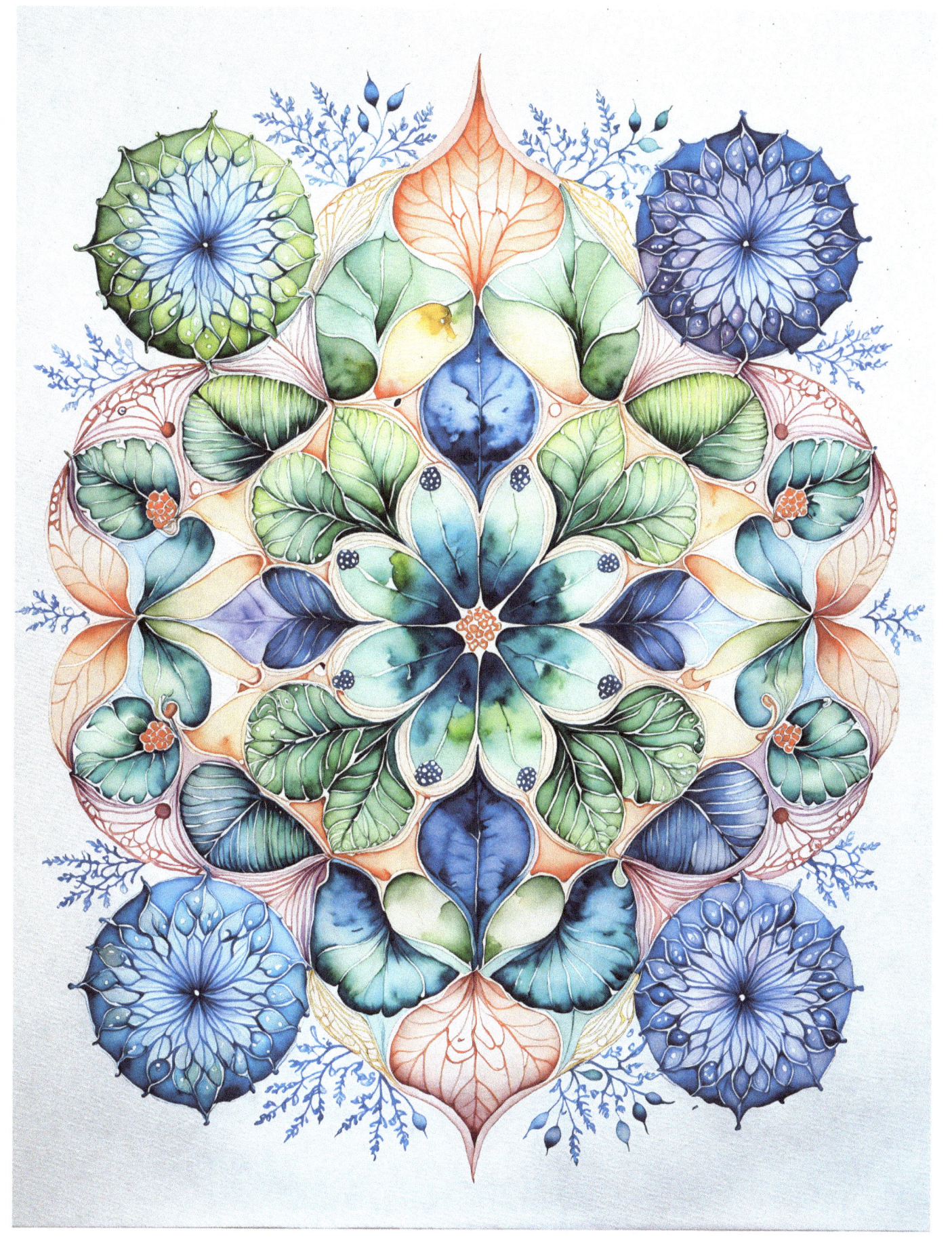

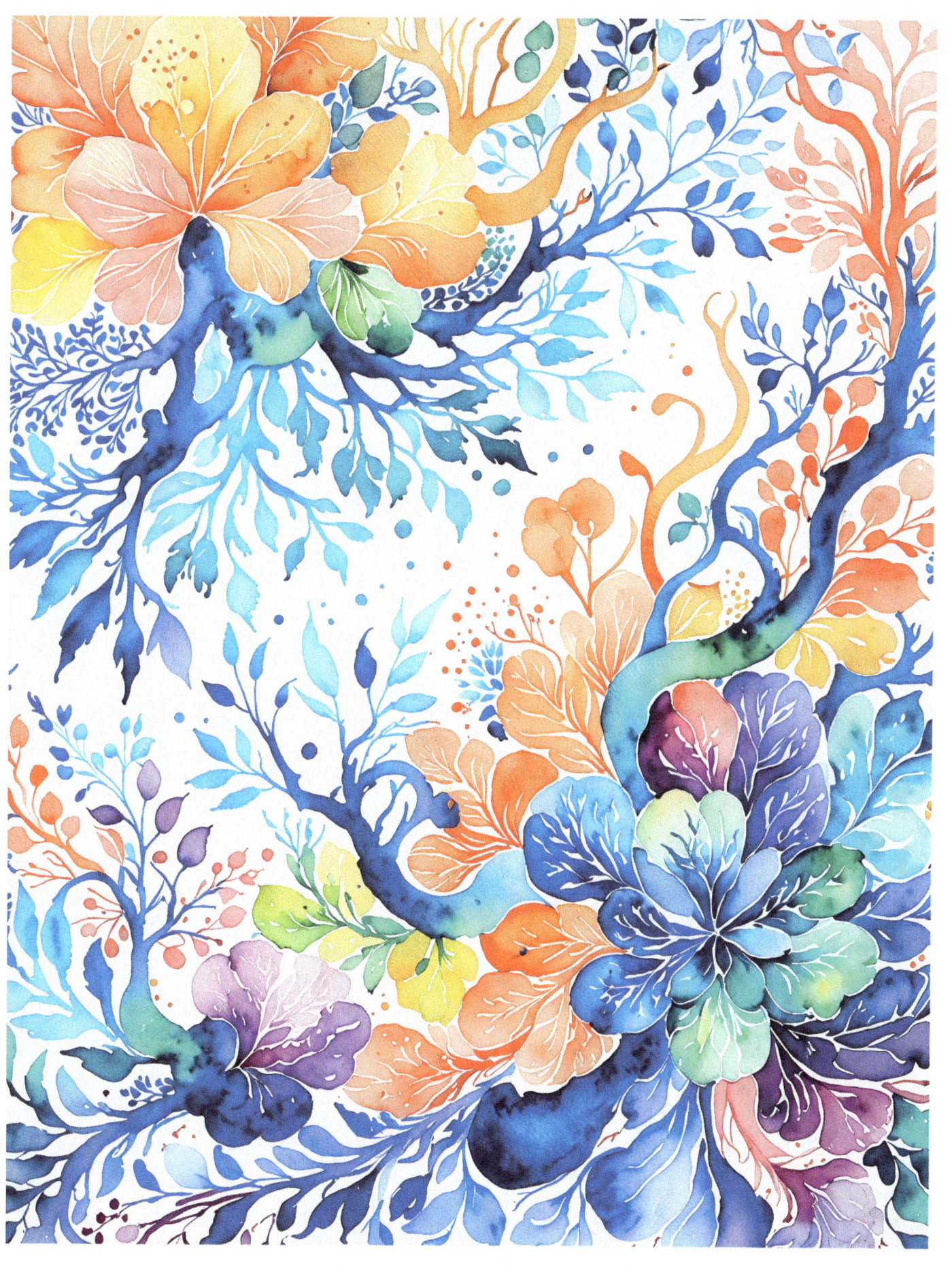

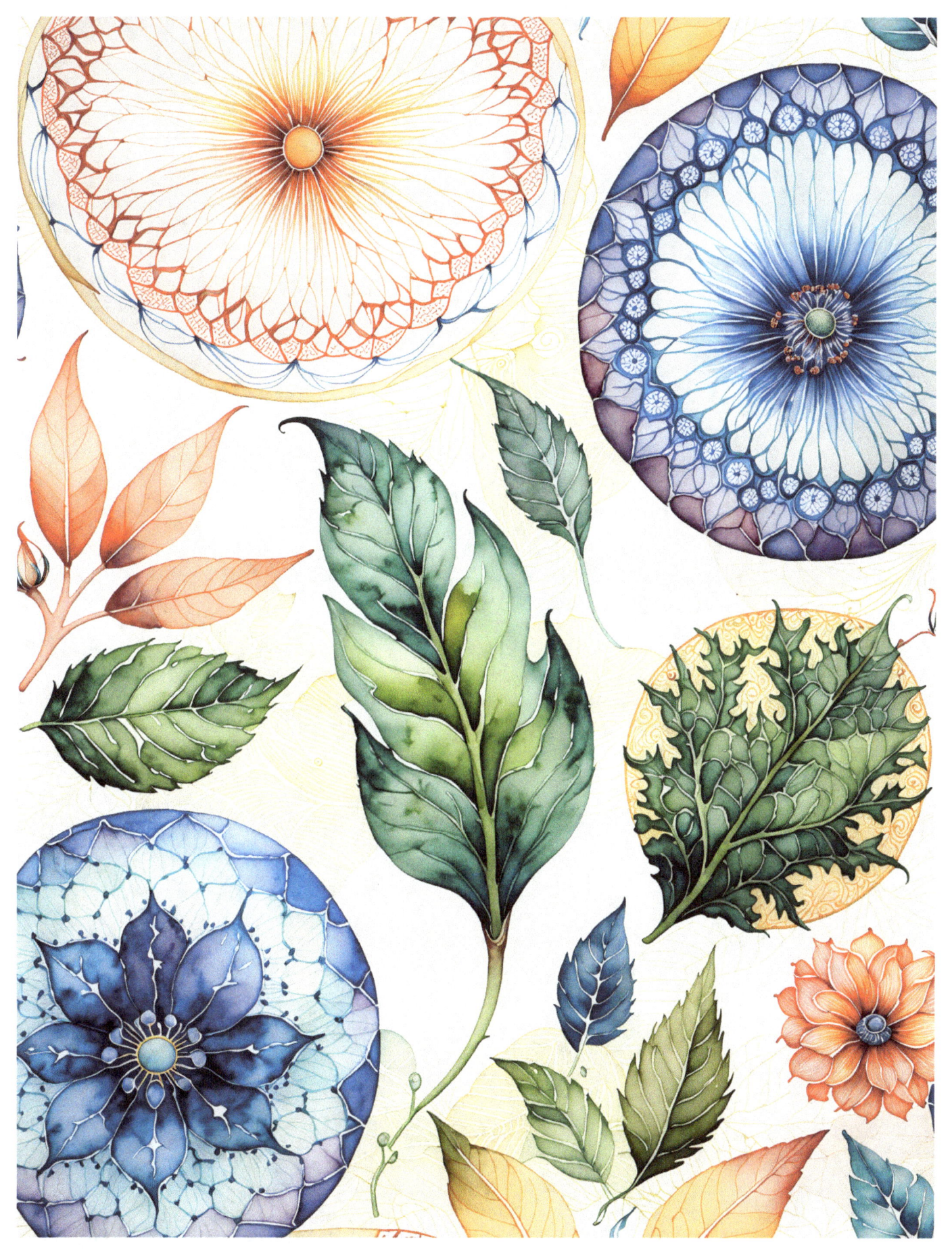

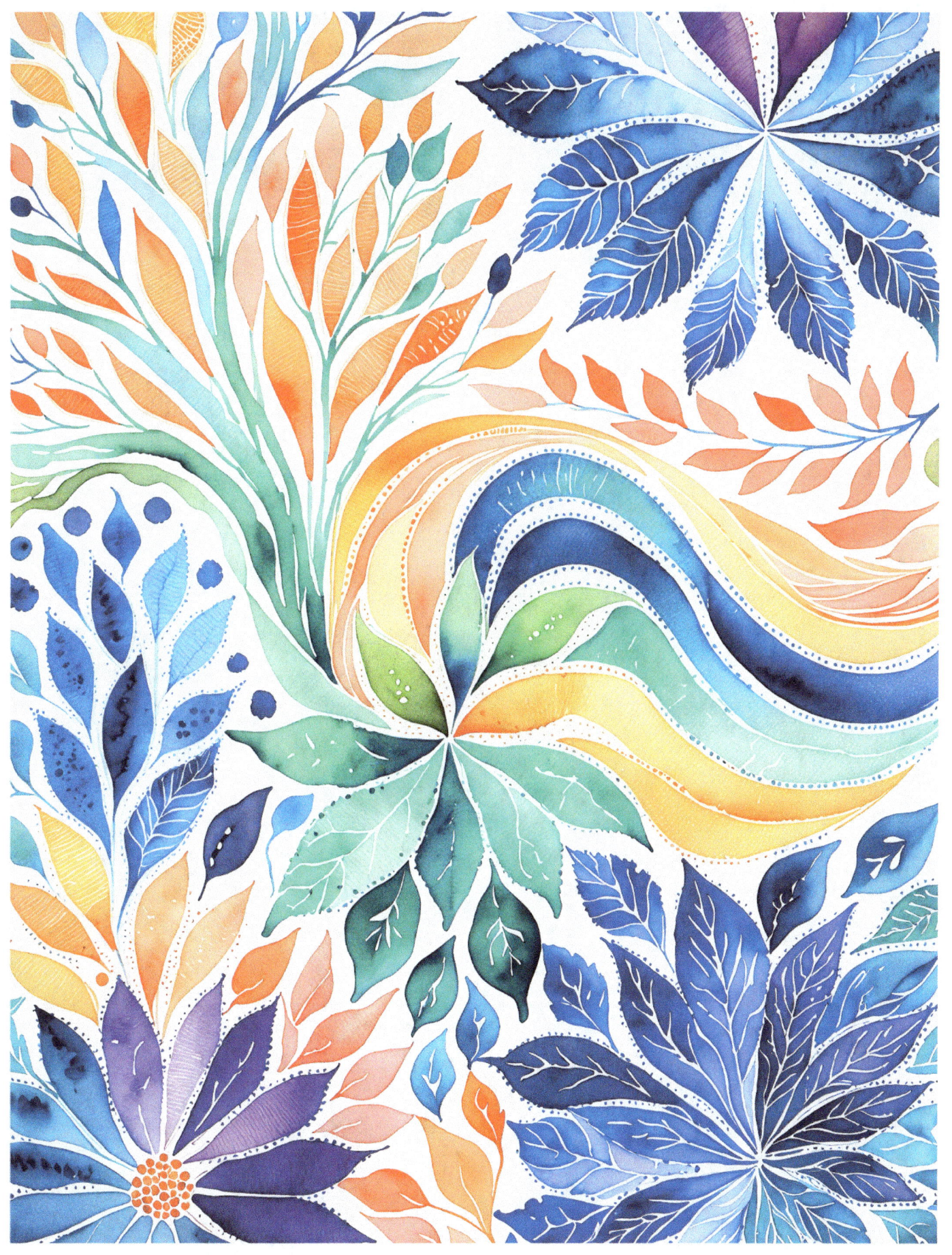

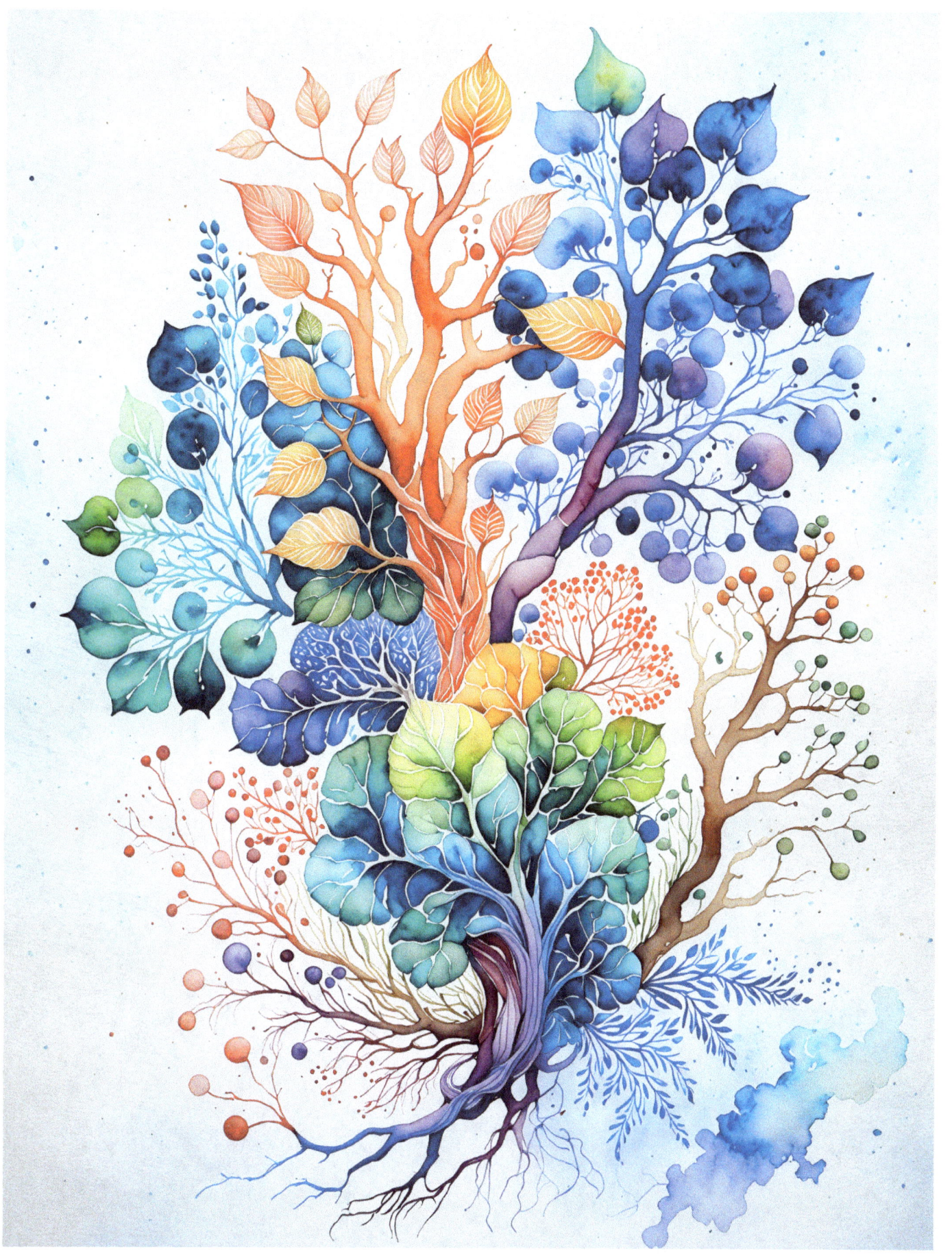

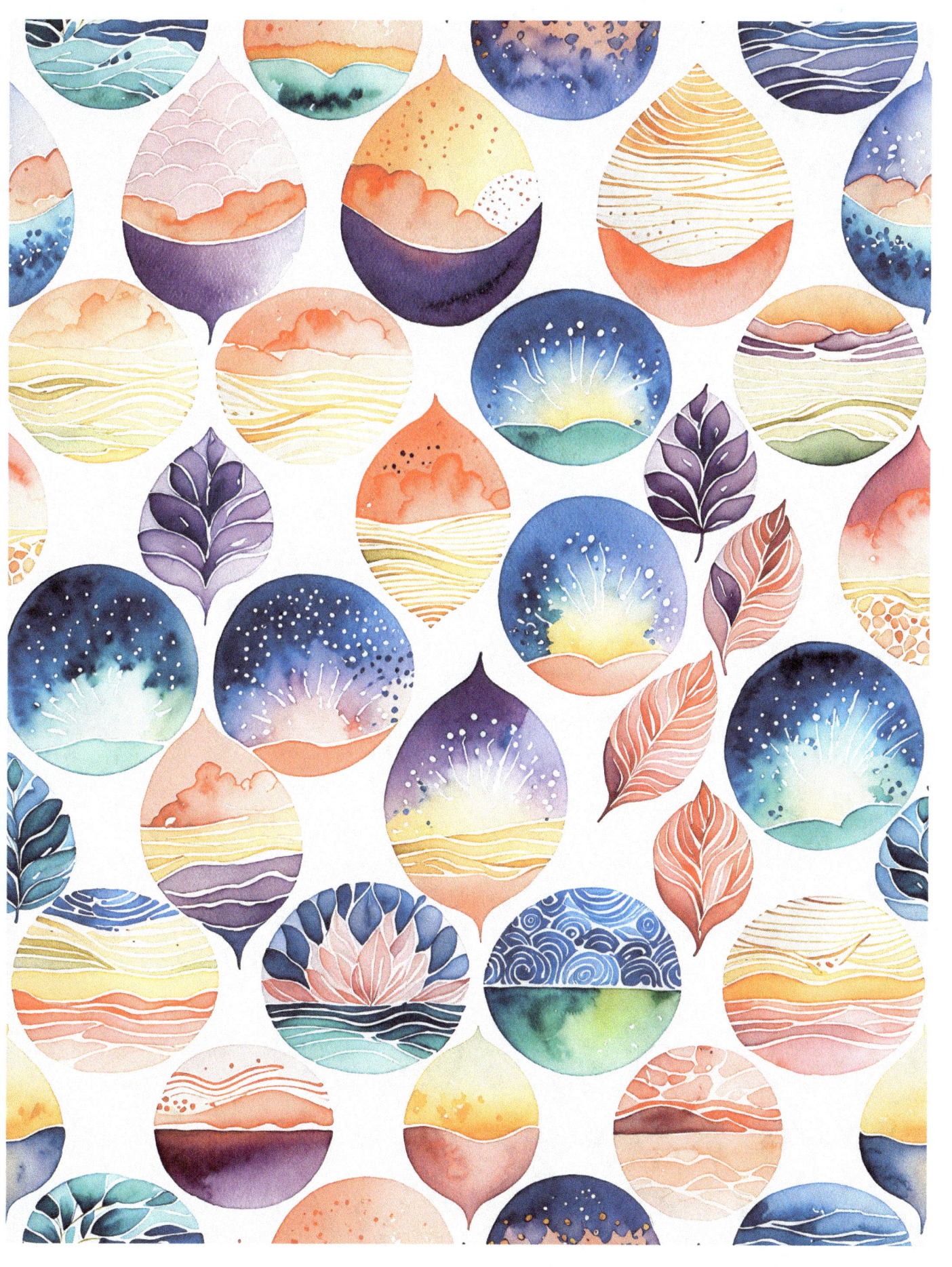

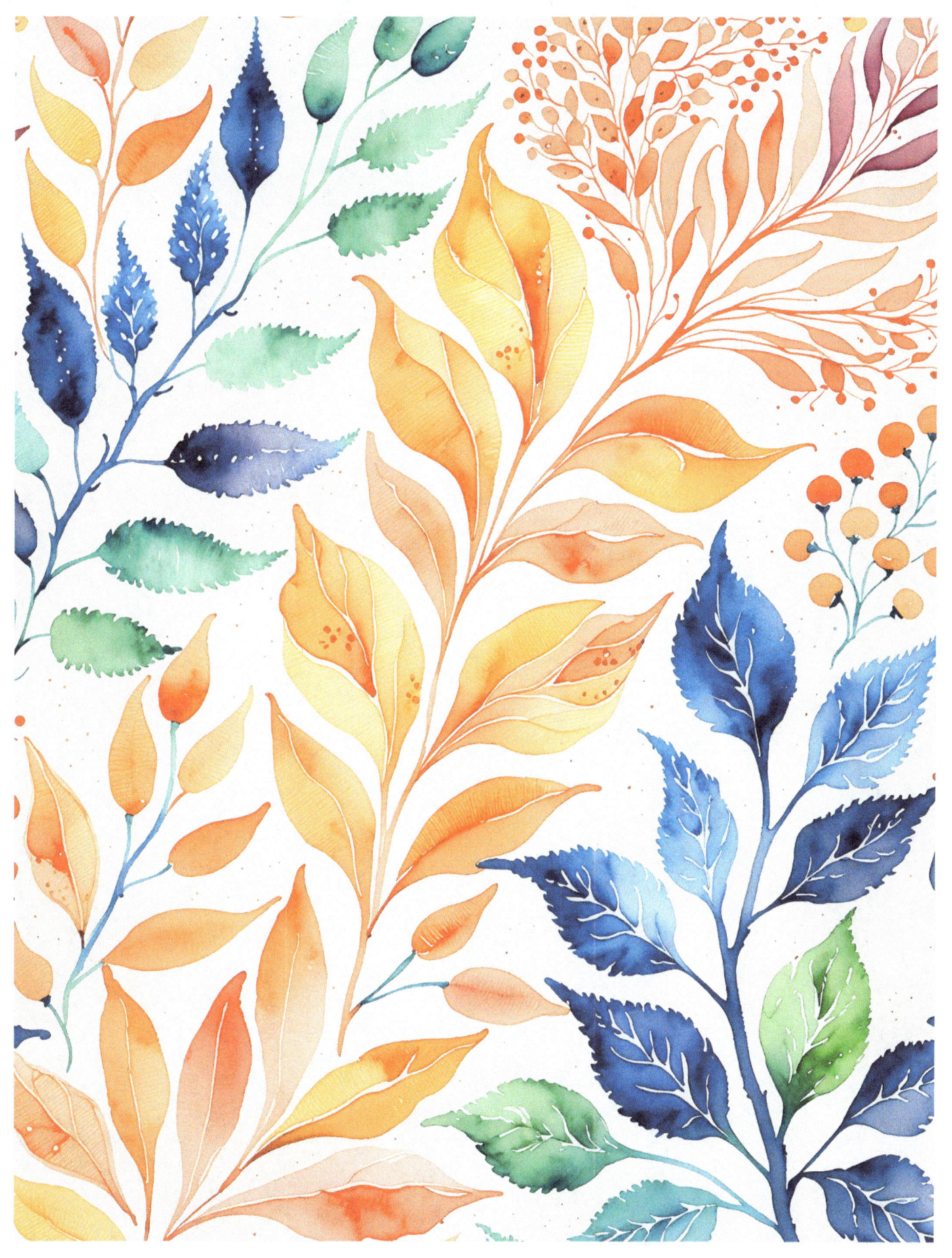

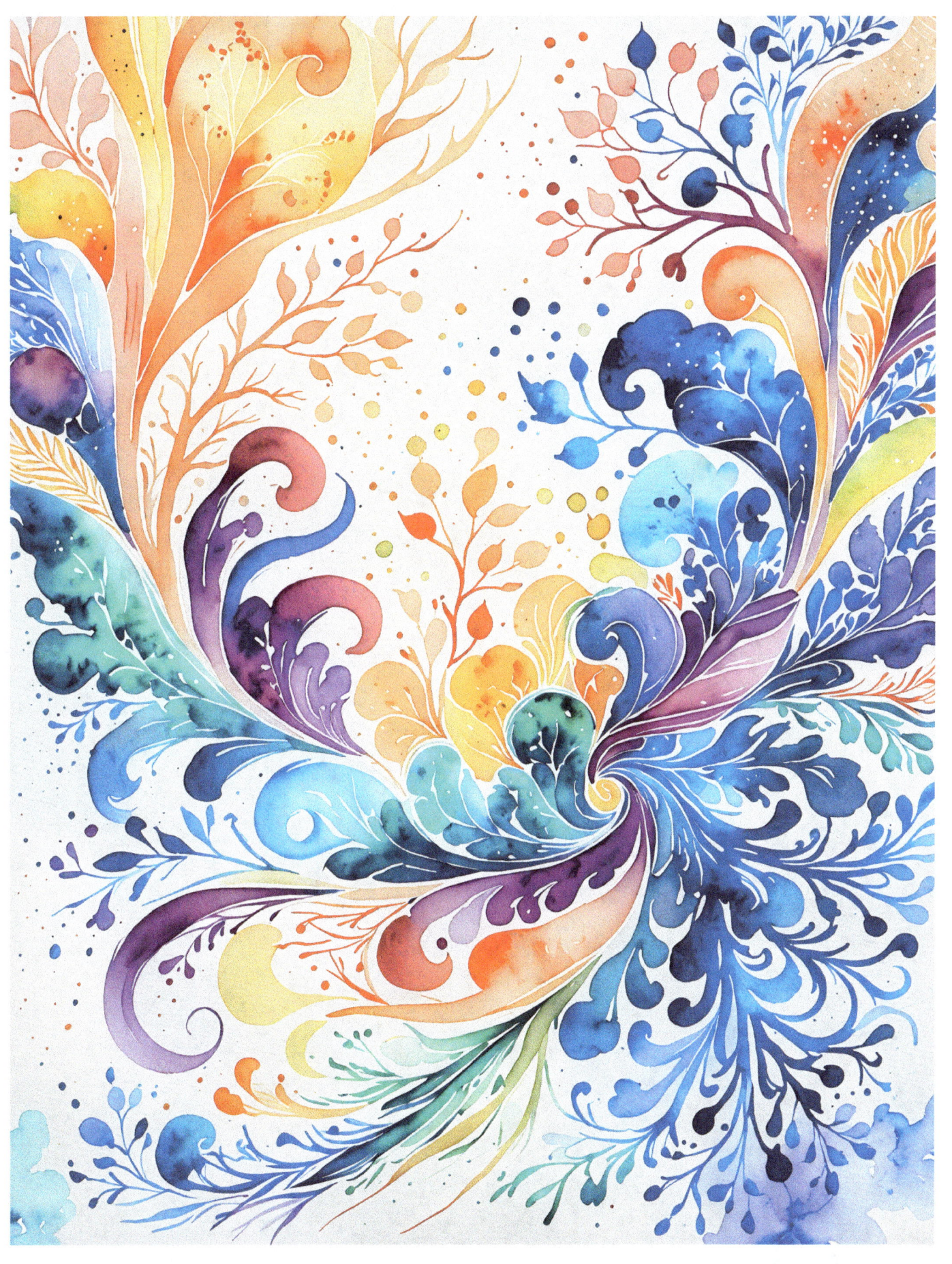

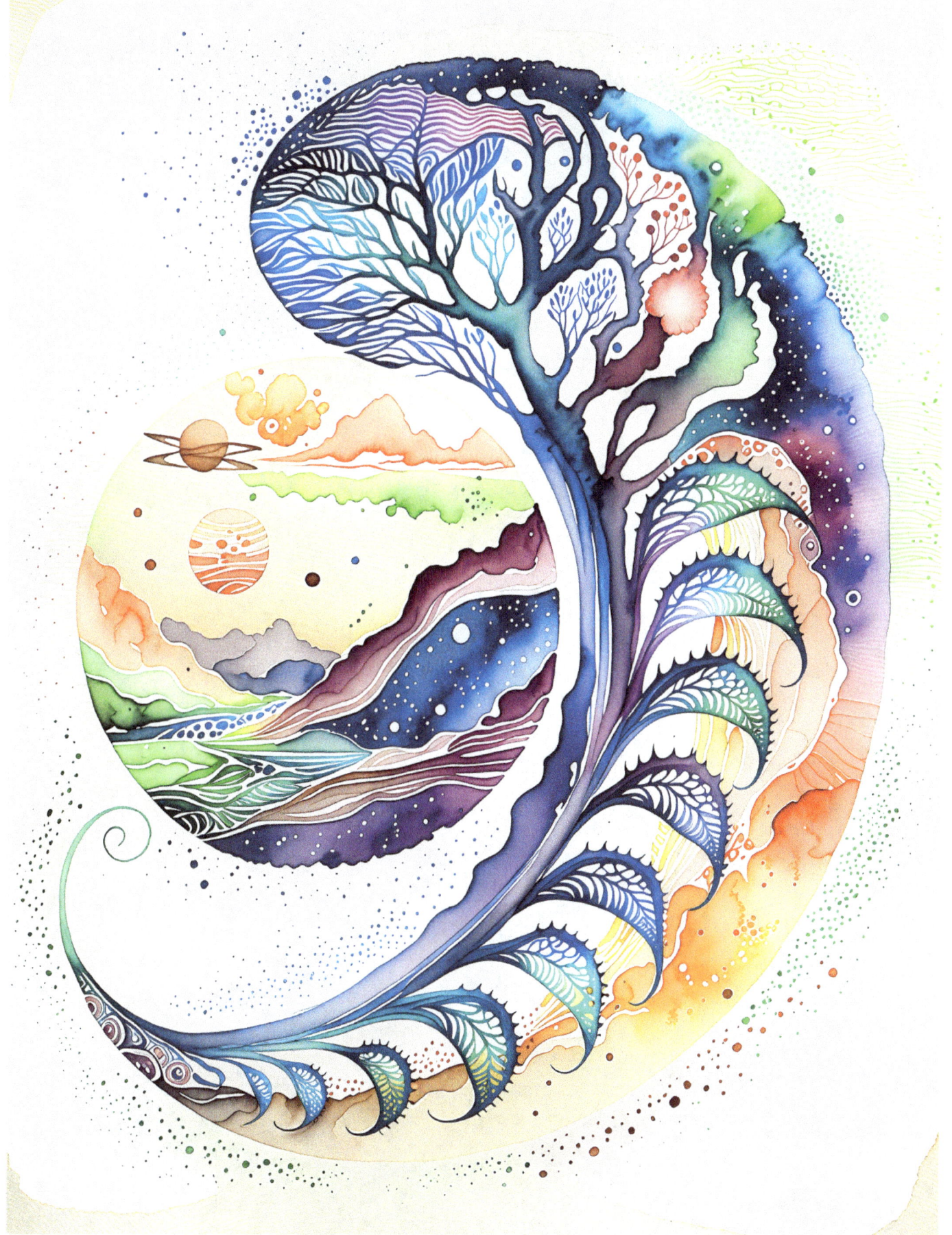

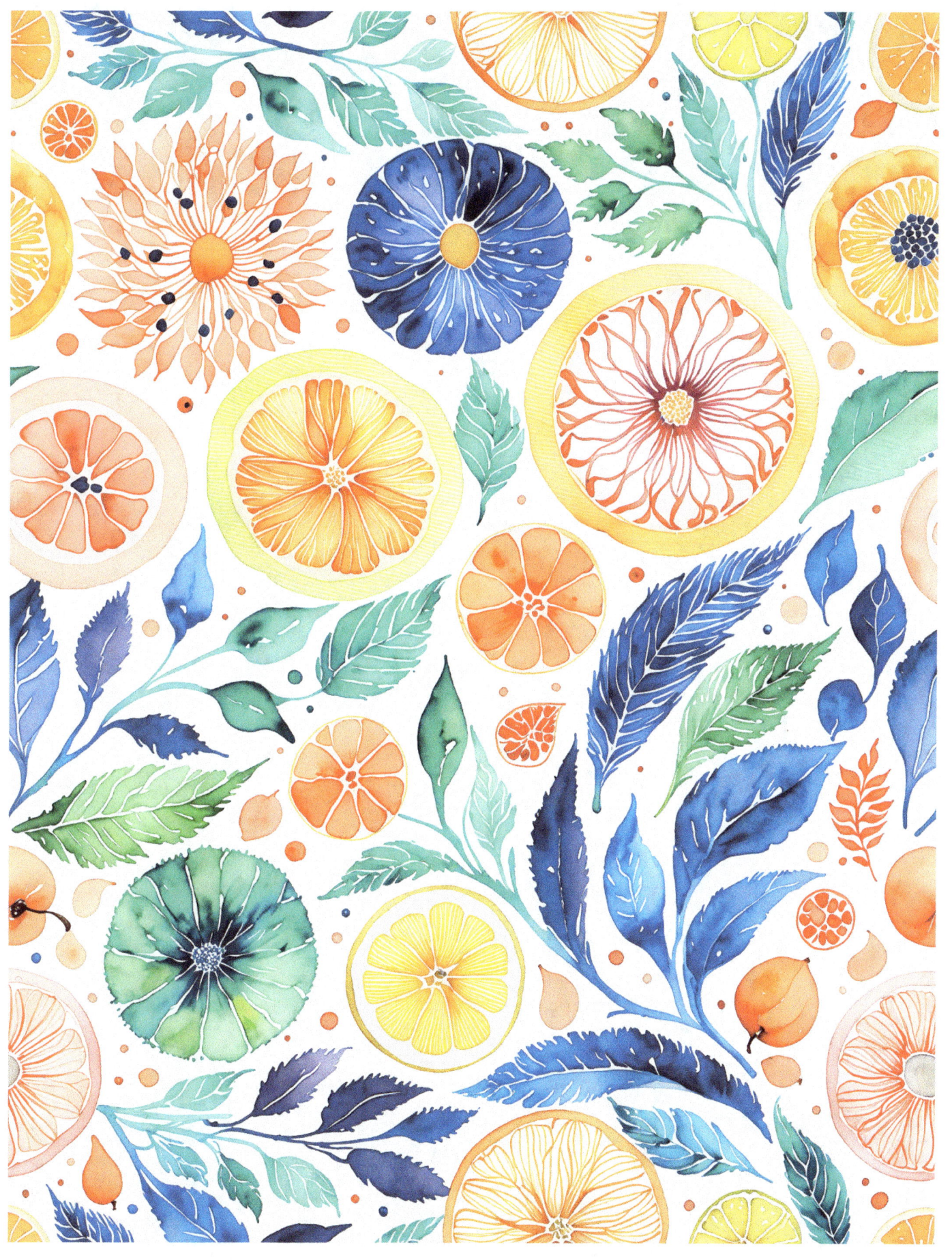

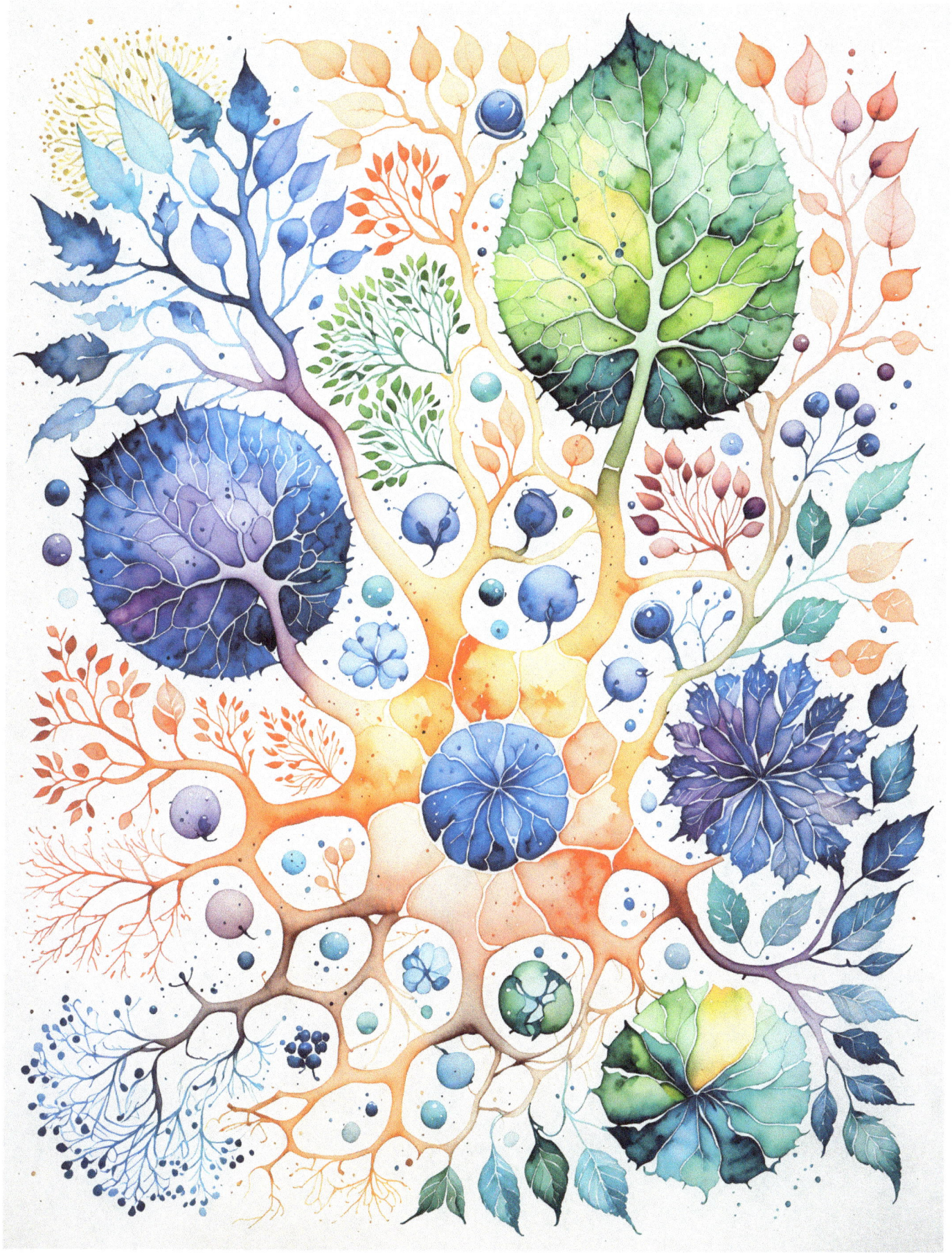

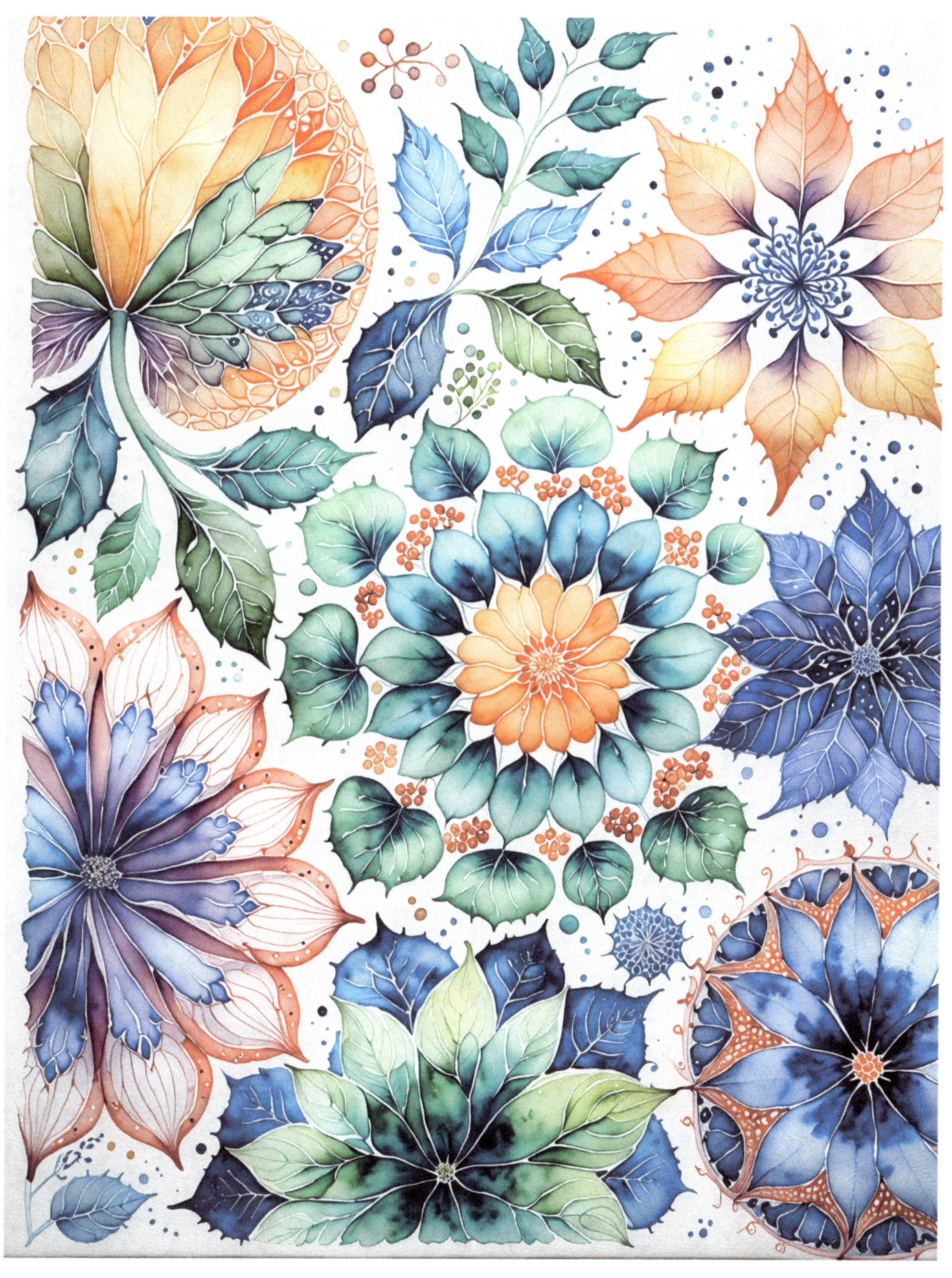

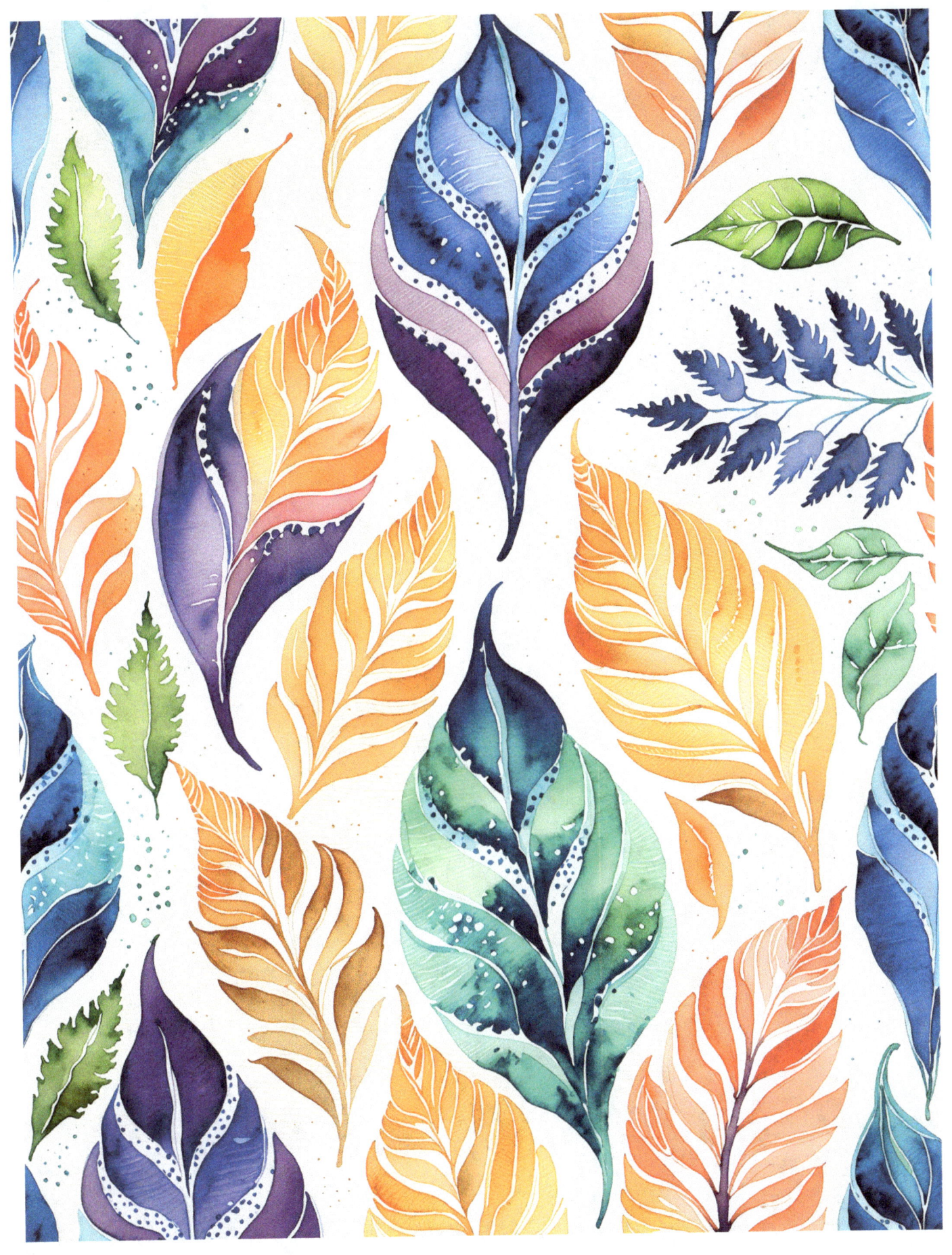

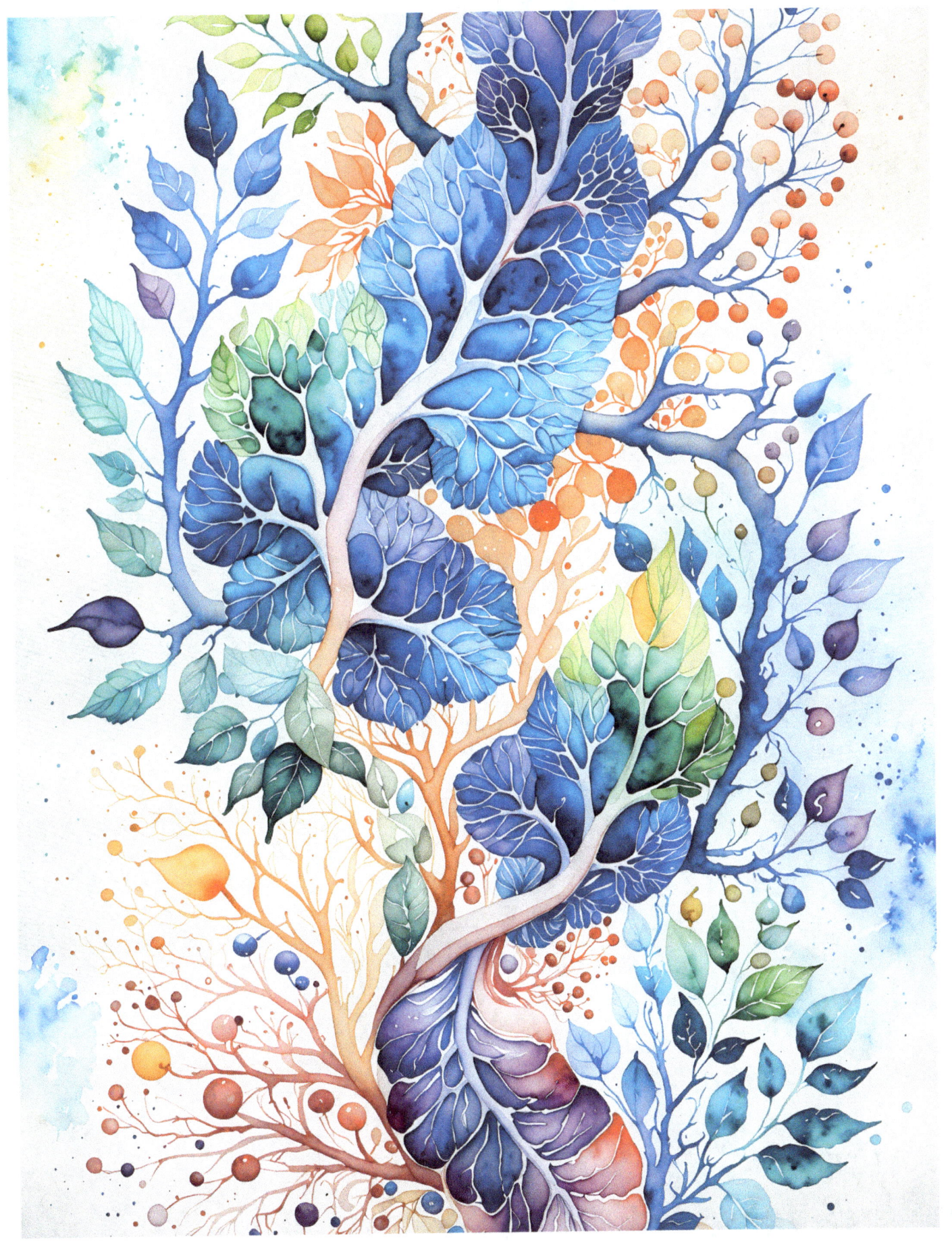

www.ingramcontent.com/pod-product-compliance
Lightning Source LLC
Chambersburg PA
CBHW062226220526
45471CB00009B/3359